LOVED
as
I AM

"In *Loved as I Am*, Sr. Miriam has blessed the Church with her powerful testimony of the victory of faith, hope, and love over the doubt, despair, and lust that cast their shadow over so many souls. Her inspiring and authentic witness is proof that God wants to write his own powerful story of redemption in each of our lives."

Jason Evert
Author of *Theology of the Body for Teens*

"*Loved as I Am* is Sr. Miriam's heartfelt testimony of her journey to healing and wholeness in Christ. This book will speak to anyone who is searching for meaning in their own lives."

Rev. Bryce Sibley
Pastor and Chaplain
Our Lady of Wisdom Church and Catholic Student Center
University of Louisiana-Lafayette

"Sr. Miriam is an authentic witness of Jesus' irresistible love. With vulnerability, honesty, and beauty, she invites each of us to experience the Lord's astonishing love—just as we are. Be prepared for a life-changing encounter."

Bob Schuchts
Author of *Be Healed*

"By weaving together the truths of the Theology of the Body and her personal journey, Sr. Miriam offers an inspiring testimony of God's loving power to heal and restore our deepest hurts. The beauty of her vulnerability opens a door of hope that, if walked through, will lead to new life."

Jake and Heather Khym
Life Restoration, Inc.

"I am convinced this little book will change many lives. The rare combination of inspiring witness, relevant scriptural reflection, and razor-sharp commentary offers powerful insights and lingering hope. Like watching a beautiful sunset, you may race through this book and then not want to finish it!"

Brian Butler
Dumb Ox Ministries

LOVED as I AM

An Invitation to Conversion, Healing, and Freedom through Jesus

Miriam James Heidland, S.O.L.T.

AVE MARIA PRESS AVE Notre Dame, Indiana

Founded in 1865, Ave Maria Press is a ministry of the United States Province of Holy Cross.

www.avemariapress.com

Paperback: ISBN-13 978-1-59471-546-4

E-book: ISBN-13 978-1-59471-547-1

Cover and text design by Andy Wagoner.

Printed and bound in the United States of America.

Library of Congress Cataloging-in-Publication Data

Heidland, Miriam James.

  Loved as I am : an invitation to conversion, healing, and freedom through Jesus / Miriam James Heidland, S.O.L.T.

    pages cm

  Includes bibliographical references.

  ISBN 978-1-59471-546-4 (pbk.) -- ISBN 978-1-59471-547-1 (ebook)

  1. Heidland, Miriam James. 2. Catholic converts--United States--Biography. 3. Nuns--United States--Biography. 4. Monastic and religious life of women--United States. I. Title.

  BX4668.H35A3 2014

  271'.97--dc23

    [B]

                              2014012304

Contents

Foreword by Christopher West   ix

Acknowledgments   xi

Introduction   xiii

Chapter 1: Tell Me Who I Am   1

Chapter 2: Show Me My Purpose   12

Chapter 3: Come and Find Me   24

Chapter 4: Mend My Broken Heart   34

Chapter 5: Untangle My Secrets   44

Chapter 6: Wipe Away My Tears   55

Chapter 7: Heal My Wounds   65

Chapter 8: Set Me Free   76

Chapter 9: Open My Heart to Love   86

Conclusion   98

Notes   101

Additional Resources   105

Foreword

It's reported that St. Teresa of Avila used to be heard whispering under her breath, "God save us from (overly) pious nuns." This great saint's prayer has certainly been answered in Sister Miriam.

I've known Sister Miriam for several years, and she is anything but the stereotypical picture of a sister. In fact, she's a wild woman—in the best sense of that word: wild in her desire for God; wild in her joy for life; wild in her pursuit of God's fire; and wild in her desire for others' healing, wholeness, and happiness. In short, Sister Miriam is a woman who has encountered infinite love. As the title of her book indicates, she knows she is "loved as she is"—and that love has transformed her.

As she candidly shares in this book, her wildness wasn't always directed in the right way. In her younger years, Sister Miriam took her passion to "an endless stream of parties and men" which left her "empty and broken." At that point in her life, you might say she was lost in her passion. Yet, her story attests to the truth spoken by St. Augustine: "He who loses himself in his passion is less lost than he who loses his passion." It is that very passion that, when we get to the deepest part of it, also leads us to the infinite passion of God, for which we are created.

Following Jesus takes nothing of our authentic humanity away from us. As Sister Miriam's story makes so clear, Christ doesn't stifle our passion; he redeems it, "untwists" it, redirecting our *desires* according to his *design* so we can reach our *destiny*: eternal bliss in an Infinity of Love that the Bible calls "the Marriage of the Lamb" (Rev 19:7).

As a sister, Miriam has chosen to "skip" the sacrament of marriage (the earthly sign that points us to heaven) in order to devote herself to *the real thing*—the eternal Marriage for which we're all destined. In this way, her whole life proclaims that *heaven is real* and it is worth selling *everything* to possess. As Sister Miriam's life shows, celibacy for the kingdom, properly lived and embraced, does not distance you from others or make you seem "aloof." It draws you closer to others and gets you all the more in touch with the real "shtuff" of life.

Sister Miriam knows well the longings, difficulties, struggles, fears, questions, and hurts of the human heart. And she knows well the journey—long, often painful, but always hopeful and incredibly rewarding—towards wholeness and happiness. It's a journey that begins with knowing I am "loved as I am."

This book is about to guide you on a healing journey. Sit back. Relax. And open wide your heart to the shower of graces coming your way.

Christopher West
Author of *Fill These Hearts: God, Sex, and the Universal Longing*

Acknowledgments

There are many people throughout my life who have shaped, formed, and encouraged me. First and foremost, I would like to thank God for his beauty, goodness, and mercy; for creating me, calling me, and never giving up on me. I would like to thank my biological parents for choosing life. To the parents who raised me, Jim (deceased) and Agnes, I love you so very much; thank you for being open to the will of God in your lives.

To Fr. Santan Pinto, S.O.L.T. (deceased); Sr. Anne Marie Walsh, S.O.L.T.; Dr. Clare Ten Eyck; Fr. Emmerich Vogt, O.P.; Julie Proctor; Christopher West; Jake Khym; and Dr. Bob Schuchts: I wouldn't be here today without you. I am so grateful for your love and kindness. Thank you to my Society of Our Lady of the Most Holy Trinity religious community; the dear staff at Ave Maria Press, especially my editor Kristi McDonald; and fellow author Lisa Hendey. Thank you for giving me a chance to share God's healing power with the world.

To the woman who is full of grace and beauty, Mary, Refuge of Sinners, thank you for saying yes to God and changing human history. Please pray for us now and at the hour of our death.

Introduction

What is the deepest desire of your heart? What stirs in your heart as a longing that burns to be fulfilled?

If you had asked me those questions many years ago, I would have told you that I wanted to be rich and famous. Had you asked me about my career aspirations when I was a teenager, I would have told you that I wanted to work for ESPN or be the CEO of a successful company. I really wanted to be someone. I wanted to make a difference in this world, and I wanted to do it in a big way. In college, I was on my way: while playing volleyball on a scholarship at a Division I university, I pursued internships at a television station, a radio station, and a public relations firm. I envisioned myself in a high-profile job with lots of travel, glamour, and money.

There is nothing inherently wrong with success, but in spite of prestigious internships, a high-level college volleyball career, and an endless stream of parties and men, I felt empty and broken. On the exterior, I probably seemed happy and content, but I was dying on the inside.

Waking up one morning after a long night of partying, I recalled all the horrible things I had done the night before. My disgust with myself and my life was piercing because I had promised myself that I was going to change, that I was going to live differently. I couldn't stand the sin that I was regularly indulging in, but no matter how good my intentions were, I kept falling right back into the same patterns. The pain was so deep that day that I curled up into a little ball on the floor of my room and wished for death. I ached for so much more than the life I was living.

It was often in the quiet moments, deep in the night, that bubbles of truth would well up to the surface of my heart. When coming home from some party or during the rare times when I was sitting in silence, a deep unhappiness would emerge. I had always thought that if I was successful enough and perfect enough, if enough people liked me and approved of me, I would be happy. But I wasn't happy—I was shattered. In my heart, I wanted to live a life of truth and beauty; I wanted a life of freedom and joy. I was very hungry for a better life, but I didn't know how to find one.

The twelve-step program for recovering alcoholics proclaims, "We are only as sick as our secrets." By the time I was twenty-one years old, I had secrets of abuse, alcohol addiction, and lust. I was a sick young woman on many levels, and I was trying to make myself feel better by seeking happiness the only way I knew how: through pleasure and self-gratification at any cost. Mainstream society tells us that religion is outdated and that there is no such thing as right or wrong—in short, that we have no need of Jesus. I had stopped attending church regularly and did whatever I wanted with my "freedom," but this did not bring me the joy I was after. All I could see were shadows and darkness, and I had no idea how to become truly free. I was stuck and sinking fast.

Yet in the midst of this darkness, a light began to shine in the barrenness of my broken heart. Authentic love gently, but directly, intervened in my life in the form of a very holy and brave Catholic priest named Fr. Santan Pinto. Father knew that my life was sinful and broken, but he did not shame me. He saw beauty in me where I saw only ugliness, and he continually encouraged me to seek an authentic life with God, rather than waste my life in sin. The friendship and fatherhood Fr. Pinto shared with me over the course of many years changed my destiny. He taught me that the ideologies the world imposes upon us are utterly false. The reality is that we are made for goodness, truth, and beauty. We long for more because we are made for more. This is humanity's calling.

Seeing Jesus Christ in this devoted man of God began to set my mind and heart free to dream and to love. This transformation from darkness into light was, and still is, a slow and sometimes painful process but worth the effort. You see, our hearts long for authentic love because we were made in and for authentic love. No amount of lust, greed, glamour, pleasure, or fame will ever satisfy us because we aren't made for falsehood and passing things. Even surrounded by the good and beautiful things of this earth, we still ache and yearn and long. We are made for eternity; we are attracted by love.

In this book, I will share my heart and my story with you, as well as biblical stories and Church teaching, hoping to illumine a path in your own heart, for God often speaks to us in the stories of others. We will explore God's original plan for the human person, the brokenness we all face, and the real hope we have for freedom and redemption.

I want you to know that Jesus Christ is real. He is real in history and he is also vibrantly real in our daily lives. He is alive. God's love for you and longing for you are real. You may not believe this, or you may feel disappointed by God and his Church. You may not want to have anything to do with God. He knows this because he knows you. He meets you and respects you wherever you find yourself. He calls. He waits. He invites. God has created us for himself, and as St. Augustine so fittingly wrote, "Our hearts are restless, O Lord, until they rest in You." The great journey of authentic love is the most challenging yet most rewarding journey you will ever make. Are you ready to step forward on this journey? Come and see.

Chapter 1

Tell Me Who I Am

In the darkness, something was happening at last. A voice had begun to sing.

—C. S. Lewis, *The Magician's Nephew*

Then God said: Let us make human beings in our image, after our likeness.

—Genesis 1:26

I still remember the smell of the middle school cafeteria in 1989. It was a combination of floor cleaner, floor wax, and whatever the lunch ladies were preparing on that particular day. As I stood in line, I scanned the crowd of kids, urgently looking for a friend to sit with. After getting my milk, hot dog, and cookie, I faced the mob of twelve- and thirteen-year-olds. I stared at the tables while trying to avoid the eyes of my classmates staring back at me.

Were they talking about me?

Did I look like a total loser standing there with no friends and no place to sit?

Could they see all the stuff in my heart that I tried so hard to hide?

I looked around in desperation. *Dang it.* None of my friends were at lunch. With all the awkwardness of a skinny, braces-wearing, insecure thirteen-year-old girl, I plopped myself down at the end of a table with people I didn't want to talk to. If I pretended they didn't exist, maybe they wouldn't talk to me either. I just wanted a place where I could be myself and not have to worry if people liked me. I didn't like who I was at that age. I didn't like what I looked like or how I felt, so out of place and uncomfortable in my own skin. Sometimes just being me felt like an utter humiliation (and sometimes it still does). When would I get it together once and for all?

Now that I'm a grown woman looking back on that experience, I see that I was simply looking for a place to call home. I realize now that the world can be a difficult place where we feel we have to wear masks, put on a good show, and take care to hide our weaknesses. Even if we excel at sports, achieve at school, or have a million online friends, sometimes we feel overwhelmingly alone and we wonder if anyone really ever *sees* us. Will we ever find someone who understands our hearts and just loves us as we are? Will we ever be truly happy? It is as if our whole lives are a quest to find a place where we belong and a happiness in which we can rest.

We go to great lengths to pursue happiness by fitting in with other people. We take up common sports, interests, and fashions. We buy the same things other people have. As we get older, we can easily put on the masks of the proper university degree, bank account balance, or politically correct service project.

And yet, our desire to fit in, belong, and be happy isn't the problem. God made us for communion and relationship, and God is ultimate happiness. Our struggle is that we spend a large portion of our lives seeking belonging and happiness in unfulfilling and often destructive ways.

Even by the end of my middle-school years, I sold out my friends by gossiping about them or leading them into dangerous situations like sneaking out at night or partying because I wanted to fit in and be liked by other people. Betraying my friends or breaking the rules my parents set up for me never brought me lasting happiness, though—it only brought me sorrow and trouble. So what is this desire for belonging and happiness that keeps rising up in our hearts?

I find politics and pop culture to be fascinating, and I can often be found listening to talk shows or the radio while out for a walk or a drive. Some time ago, I was watching a talk show debate on a news channel, and one of the guests said something I will never forget. He was talking about how American citizens are very ignorant of the foundations of our country and are therefore ignorant of what it really means to be American. The guest said, *"If we don't know where we came from and where we are going, we will be easily manipulated."* This profound remark can easily be applied to the spiritual life.

If we are honest with ourselves, we can see that something is amiss within our hearts and in society at large. We don't seem to know where we came from and we have no idea where we are going. We are very confused amidst all the voices of the world that tell us that happiness lies in acquiring possessions, wealth, and popularity; and these same voices often try to push God out of the picture. They say that God sucks the fun out of everything and that true freedom exists in doing whatever we want, however we want.

Yet something doesn't add up. Today's American society is vastly more affluent than the rest of the world. Untold pleasures are within reach of all of our fingertips. So why is suicide one of the leading causes of death for people ages fifteen to fifty-four?[1] Why do people seem to be more violent, restless, and addicted than ever? No matter how much stuff or status we acquire, it never seems to satisfy the deepest yearnings of our hearts. We long for more than material possessions and passing sexual encounters that leave the heart broken and empty. Isn't there more to life than this? There is, and we can find the answer we are looking for in the life of Jesus Christ.

Have you ever wondered why Jesus wasn't confused about who he was? (He didn't freak out in the lunch line over his lack of friends, or use people for his own pleasure.) How was he so comfortable with himself that he could joyfully endure ridicule, misunderstandings, sufferings, and ultimately crucifixion? Why didn't he bend to conform to the opinions of other people as we so often do or feel sorry for himself when things didn't go his way? The gospels reveal that Jesus touched and healed lepers (Mt 8:3), ate with unsavory sinners (Mt 9:10), and encountered bitter opposition from the powerful people of his time (Mt 12:14). Why was Jesus so free to love and speak the truth? Because *he knew who he was.* Breathe that in for one second. *He knew who he was.* Jesus lived his entire life from his true identity.

Jesus knew he was the beloved Son of God. He knew where he came from and where he was going. As broken humans, you and I often base our identity on what other people think about us. Jesus' identity was based not on the passing opinions of other people but on the eternal foundation of God the Father. Jesus shows us by the way he lived his life how a beloved child of God can live in our world. And we share the same identity as Jesus: we, too, are children of God. The answers to the questions of who we are, where we came from, and where we are going, are actually quite simple.

The Catechism of the Catholic Church (the giant green book you might be using as a paperweight or a bug-killer) has a really helpful glossary in the back. If you look up *person, human,* you will find this concise but rich definition: "The human individual, made in the image of God; not some thing but some one, a unity of spirit and matter, soul and body, capable of knowledge, self-possession, and freedom, who can enter into communion with other persons—and with God" (CCC Glossary). That's a lot to absorb right from the start. I will interpret this definition throughout the book, but I want to begin here to reveal the beauty of who we are as women and men in the secure plan of God.

The first part of the definition tells us that our deepest longing for belonging reflects the reality that every human being is made in the image and likeness of God (Gn 1:26). It is here that we find our true identity as children of God. Every person, no matter the circumstances of their conception or birth, is made in the image and likeness of God and is meant to live, love, and thrive. (You'll learn later why the circumstances of one's birth matters so much to me.) This simply means that your *being* is very good. You are made in the image and likeness of God. You are his son or daughter, and God doesn't make mistakes or have accidents. He knows what he is doing at all times, and he is not surprised by anything.

We are all familiar with the family photos sent out every year in Christmas cards. Pictures may show people on the beach looking perfect or dressed up as Santa (or feature a terrified kid looking at Santa), or perhaps the children are arranged in a living nativity scene. It's cute and often funny. There is one family in particular that I look forward to hearing from every Christmas. Their family photo is stunning! The entire family is gorgeous! Their photo looks like it fell out of a fashion magazine. Everyone in the family, from the mother and father all the way down to the youngest child, looks similar, and all are equally beautiful. In fact, the children look so much like the parents that if I see the kids out in public somewhere, I know which family they belong to because they look so much like their parents. The kids bear the image of their father and mother in many diverse ways.

This is a human-scale analogy to help us understand what it means that we are created in the image and likeness of God. Just as we can know a bit about the parents by looking at their children, we can know a bit about God the Creator by looking at his creation. We are the only creatures that God makes in his image and likeness (Gn 1:26). As human beings, male and female, we are *the* crown of creation—it's not the polar bear or the sea squirt that reigns supreme.

After creating humanity, God looks at all the things he has created and pronounces them to be "very good" (Gn 1:31). We are very good because we are created in the image and likeness of God who is Goodness Himself. We can know and love because God knows and loves. The *best* of our knowing and loving here on earth is only a splinter of the perfection of how God knows and loves eternally. He made us, we belong to him, and we long for him whether we realize it or not. Our belonging is ultimately found in the One who loves us, and it is foreshadowed here on earth by the love of our family and friends. Our desire to belong, to fit in and find happiness, is really a search for our eternal home—heaven. We desire happiness because we desire heaven. In heaven we will rest in the ecstatic, never-ending joy of realizing who we truly are: God's beloved sons and daughters.

I don't know about you, but sometimes when I look in the mirror in the morning, I don't find my reflection to be too pleasant. Even though I have been a religious sister for many years, I still need God to remind me who I am. One morning not too long ago, I was feeling pretty down about myself on a number of levels. When I arrived at Mass and plopped myself in the pew, I was hardly joyful or living out of my true identity as God's daughter. After an hour of self-pity, I genuflected after Mass had ended and made my way to the back of the church.

Near the door, an elderly woman stopped me and introduced me to her five-year-old granddaughter. As I bent down to greet this beautiful little girl, she looked up at me with her big eyes full of wonder and said, "You look like a princess." Needless to say, her sweet words pierced me to the heart for a number of reasons. She was reminding me of something I had forgotten in my fog of self-absorption. She was reminding me that a princess isn't a girl who is spoiled or snotty. A princess in the truest definition is a daughter of the king. I had forgotten that I am not the sum of my triumphs, failures, and faults; my deepest identity is that I am God's daughter. That is a relationship that no one can take away from me . . . or from you.

Sometimes people think that because I am a religious sister, I must have grown up in a perfect family with a perfect upbringing or maybe I at least came out of the womb glowing, with a glittery company of angels marking my arrival to planet Earth. Not quite! I will share my story throughout this book, but suffice it for now to say that I did not grow up knowing that I was created in the image and likeness of God, as his beloved daughter. I did not know that God loved me more completely than I could ever imagine. I did grow up Catholic: I went to church every Sunday with my mom and dad, and my brother and I attended classes to fulfill the requirements to receive the sacraments. Somehow, though, this deeper reality—that at the core of my being was a great calling and belonging as a true daughter of God the Father—never penetrated my heart. Catholicism for me was a list of duties, obligations, and prohibitions.

I didn't see or understand God as my loving Father who watches over me and speaks to me in my heart. I saw him as the "policeman in the sky" who notes everything I do wrong and who was overwhelmingly disappointed with me no matter how much I try. I felt that he would love me only when I was a "good girl" and that his love was conditional. If I performed well, he would love me. If I made mistakes or failed, then he would not love me as much. I did not think he knew me as I truly was and, even more disheartening, I did not think he even cared. This broken way of seeing God would haunt me for a very long time, especially as my life grew more dark and sinful. How could I believe in and trust a God of whom I was afraid? How could a faith that seemed rule-based and boring set me on fire? I had no idea. Remember the quote from the talk show guest? *"If we don't know where we came from and where we are going, we will be easily manipulated."* Welcome to many years of my life. Thankfully, love intervened in some of my darkest hours and still continues to do so.

Prayer: God, please come meet me in the place where I am right now. You know my heart; I don't have to pretend with you. Father me as I have never been fathered before. Come show me who you truly are and how beloved I am to you. Come speak to me as your child in your tender and compassionate love. Amen.

Questions for Deeper Reflection:

Answer as honestly as you can and bring your answers, desires, and fears to God.

- What are some of the deep longings of my heart? What are some of my greatest desires?

- In what ways do I try to fit in with others? Are any of these ways destructive to myself or others?

- When I am honest with myself, how do I see God? Do I see him as distant or removed? Is he uninterested or uncaring? Is he loving, kind, and compassionate? (Often we will find within our hearts a complex mix of ideas and feelings about God's intentions toward us.)

- What is my story in relationship to God? How have I experienced him in my life?

Chapter 2

Show Me My Purpose

---

*I am somebody because God don't make
no junk.*

> —Ethel Waters, *His Eye Is on the Sparrow*

*Before I formed you in the womb I knew
you, before you were born I dedicated
you.*

> —Jeremiah 1:5

In the initial stages of my formation as a religious
sister from 1998 to 2002, I was sent for three years
with many other postulants and novices to our mission in Subiaco, Italy, which is just outside the city
of Rome. Hundreds of years before, St. Benedict had
fled to this countryside to escape the depravity of
the city. We had many interesting adventures during
our stay, and I found Italians and their culture to be
deeply beautiful. Our time there brought us many
challenges but many hidden treasures as well.

During one year, I accompanied one of our
sisters into Rome twice a week because she
needed physical therapy to recover from a serious injury. While she was at her appointments, I
would sometimes roam (no pun intended) about

the surrounding neighborhoods. One afternoon, I stumbled upon the church of San Luigi dei Francesi. Entering, I saw many people walking around looking at the architecture and art, but something in the far corner of the church caught my attention. A light kept blinking on and off, and a lot people were gathered in that area, gazing at something that I couldn't see from the church entry.

Keenly interested, I walked toward the gaggle of people, who were quietly whispering to one another while looking at the wall. When I arrived at the spot, I saw that the object of everyone's interest was the original Caravaggio painting *The Calling of St. Matthew.* It took my breath away. I stood transfixed by the utter beauty, power, and stillness of that incredible work of art.

The only thing that astonished me more than the painting was the fact that the light shining upon it was operated by a coin machine, so you could only see the painting for a few minutes at a time after inserting some coins into the slot. During one's meditation and study of the painting, the light would often go out, and then people in the crowd would have to rummage in their pockets to produce more coins. Only in Italy would a great work of art be illuminated by a coin-operated light!

I returned to that church day after day to gaze at the painting, and even now it still pierces my heart to see it. This transcendent work of art was created by my favorite artist, Michelangelo Merisi da Caravaggio. He was a brilliant but troubled soul who was gifted beyond measure but who struggled with his fallen humanity his entire life.[1] In fact, he spent the last few years of his life in exile because he murdered someone in a bar fight. I love the play of light and darkness in his paintings, the earthiness of his subjects, the raw humanity revealed for all to see. How could something so beautiful come from the hands of a man so broken? How does beauty still gush forth from us who are so imperfect? Where does this beautiful love come from?

In the last chapter, we quoted the *Catechism*'s definition of *human person*, which contains two important truths: (1) that every human person possesses the nobility of being made in the image and likeness of God, being his sons and daughters; and (2) the human person is some*one*, not some*thing*. This truth has amazing consequences. It means that the human person is never to be used as a means to someone else's end. It means that all people deserve to be loved for who they are, not for what they do or for whatever pleasure they provide for others. Pope John Paul II writes, "Anyone who treats a person as the means to an end does violence to the very essence of the other. . . . We must never treat a person as a means to an end."[2]

We instinctively dislike being used by other people and have a natural distaste for people who try to use us. This reality can easily be seen in kids. At the after-school daycare where I worked for many years, we had time set aside every day for homework and study. Some of the kids worked very hard on their homework, and they did not want other students to copy their work or steal their answers. It was not uncommon to see the kids place tall barriers around their homework so others could not copy their answers.

If we do not like to be used for homework, we certainly do not like being used for darker purposes. Much of the brokenness we see in the world today is the result of human beings using one another as a means to an end rather than loving the other person and upholding the dignity and beauty of that person, who is made in the image and likeness of God. Sometimes the brokenness masquerades as "progress," "choice," or "freedom," but the fruit is always the same: more brokenness.

Even if we struggle for love in broken ways that result in using one another, in our heart of hearts we want to be loved for who we are, not merely for what we give others or what we do for others. Maybe all of us have had the experience of being used by someone else in big or small ways, and it leads our hearts to cry out, "Doesn't anyone see me for who I am and love me for who I am?"

Part of the desire to love and to be loved comes from the fact that we all want to be happy; that is the natural desire of the human heart. St. Augustine writes, "We all want to live happily; in the whole human race there is no one who does not assent to this proposition, even before it is fully articulated" (*CCC* 1718). We do what we do, for better or for worse, because we want to be happy. And we are meant as human beings to love and to be loved.

Choosing true and authentic love of God, ourselves, and others will lead us to happiness. Choosing disregard of God, lust, and use of others will only lead to unhappiness. There really are only two options: serve God and live in authentic love, or serve the Evil One and live in selfishness. This whole life on earth is a battle between these two choices.

Before I entered religious life, I thought I had "loved" the boyfriends I had dated. Looking back on those many years, though, I see that I was mostly interested in serving myself and having my emotional needs gratified at their expense. I dressed immodestly to get the attention of men, having no concern about how my provocative behavior might affect their earthly and eternal destiny. I wasn't concerned about the plan God had for the lives of these men or for my own life. My brokenness was manifested in selfishness and self-centeredness.

A life of selfishness is not a happy one. I may have gotten what I wanted on a number of occasions, but it didn't bring the real security and happiness I longed for. I did not live a life of peace and serenity, but a life of grasping and calculation. Often our struggles in life stem from conflict in the deepest parts of our humanity.

Could we not all utter the same words as St. Paul, who wrote, "I do not do the good I want, but I do the evil I do not want" (Rom 7:19)? Life on earth is often a struggle because we are at war with ourselves as a result of sin. Our bodies and our senses seem to lead us into sin, and so we experience a great dissonance within ourselves. Yet it is through and within our bodies that we carry out the mission of love. What a quandary! As human beings we are a union of soul *and* body (remember the *Catechism* definition), and this is a very beautiful thing. This union was created by God and is "very good." We are not souls who are trapped in a body, nor are we merely material beings or enlightened animals. Our souls and our bodies belong together; one is not complete without the other.

Many of us have lamented this union because so often it seems, well, disjointed. This side of the fall in the Garden of Eden, it is indeed a struggle and a battle, but "from the beginning, it was not so" (Mt 19:8). It wasn't until I began to study Pope John Paul II's teachings on the Theology of the Body[3] during my formation in religious life that I realized I was deeply broken in how I saw my body and soul. I had spent many years trying to be as "spiritual" as

I could possibly be, all the while hating my body because it seemingly got me into trouble all the time. I would think to myself, "If I could only be more spiritual and dump this earthly weight of my flesh I would be holier." But to hate the humanity that God gave to me and be redeemed with his own blood is heresy, not holiness. Hatred of our bodies and the material world with all its messiness is only a façade that hides a deeper pain.

God loves humanity—he loves our bodies. He loves them so much that he took on a body himself, beginning as an embryo and growing to full, mature manhood. Jesus often put his hands on people; he touched the sick and suffering and embraced children. He was not afraid of his humanity. The truth is that *all* parts of us must be surrendered to God for redemption: our spirits, souls, and bodies. Do we do things with our bodies that are sinful and broken? Yes, we do. Do we do things with our minds and emotions that are sinful and broken? Most certainly. All of us need to be healed and reordered, but we are called to redemption in these areas, not to destruction of what God has created.

This serves as a reminder that our bodies will be reunited with our souls at the final judgment (*CCC* 366). We will have resurrected bodies for all eternity, and Jesus leads the way for all those who follow him. This is why St. Paul writes, "But now Christ has been raised from the dead, the first fruits of those who have fallen asleep" (1 Cor 15:20). The Resurrection of Jesus is not just a nice story we tell children on Easter Sunday; it completely changes every aspect of creation. It is powerful, life-altering, and the hope of our deepest dreams. Death has no more power over us because Jesus suffered, died, and rose from the dead. The world will never be the same.

Back to Italy. I learned a lot there, both in my head and within my heart. One of our assignments included serving children at a preschool. It was highly entertaining for me to watch four-year-old kids converse, using all the Italian hand gestures, and to see them play "church procession" as one of their favorite games.

A fellow sister, who was by far the favorite of all the children, quietly challenged me by her example to examine my arrogant and egotistical ways. Where I was proud, she was simple. Where I wanted to assert myself, she was humble. It was an ongoing encounter for me with my own masks and façades. Watching the way she loved the children was a lesson for me that I will never forget. Her artistry and kindness won the hearts of all the kids.

One day, as we all gathered around the television to watch a movie on the life of Jesus, one of the little girls climbed onto this sister's lap and settled in. When the scene showed Jesus speaking to his disciples, the sister said to the little girl, "Look, it's Jesus! There he is."

The little girl replied, "That's not Jesus."

The sister said, "Yes, that's him. Look, he's talking to his disciples."

But the little girl shook her head: "No, that's not Jesus. Jesus is like you."

Even as I write this, that memory brings tears to my eyes. The sincerity of that little girl in bestowing the deepest compliment possible completely blew me away. When was the last time you were mistaken for Jesus? As our lives are redeemed and joined to the life of Jesus, the world around us changes because the face of Christ is made manifest. Or as St. Paul simply states, "Whenever a person turns to the Lord the veil is removed. . . . And where the Spirit of the Lord is, there is freedom" (2 Cor 3:16–17).

You are here now on this earth with a purpose. You did not come to earth a hundred years ago, and you most likely will not be here a hundred years from now. Imagine this as you hold this book in your hands. You, as you are, have never been in existence before. From the beginning of time to the end of time, if God ever stops creating new people, he will never recycle or recreate you. There is no one like you. There is also no one whom God loves like you. He does not compare you to your older brother or younger sister. His love is not divided. He does not wish you were a boy if you are a girl. To him, you are not "unplanned" or an "accident." You are meant to be here on this earth. You are willed to be here, and you have a great destiny.

God knew what he was doing in creating you in all your beauty and nobility. You are loved and delighted in by God. If you think for a second about the billions of people who have lived and died on this earth and the many more people whom God will create, the sheer creativity and blessing of God is staggering. The person in your life whom you love the most is made in the image and likeness of God; so is the person whom you dislike, as well as the person who has hurt you. Every single person ever created is made in the image and likeness of God and is loved and delighted in by God. No one will ever be recycled, recreated, or reincarnated. The exquisite creation that is you will never be duplicated. Your preciousness is unrepeatable, no matter what flaws or struggles you may have. Every single person is created by Love, for love. In that Love, which is God, is found tremendous beauty. Let that beauty flow in your life.

Prayer: *Father, thank you for creating me as a unique person. Thank you for creating me in love and for love. Please help me to live the purpose of my life, to live in true love, and to truly love others. Thank you for creating my body and soul. May I allow your healing grace to flow into the areas of my body and soul that are wounded, and may the grace of the Resurrection of Jesus become living and active in my life. Amen.*

Questions for Deeper Reflection:

Answer as honestly as you can and bring your answers, desires, and fears to God.

- What do I believe about the purpose of my life? Do I believe that I was created by Love and for love as unique, precious, and unrepeatable? Do I believe I was an "accident" or the product of chance?

- In what ways do I treat other people in my life as some*one*, and what are the ways I treat them as some*thing*? Am I allowing people in my life to use me so I won't feel rejected or neglected?

- How do I view my body and my humanity? What about myself do I reject? What characteristics do I accept and love?

- Which areas in my life need healing so I can love myself as God loves me? Be specific.

Chapter 3

Come and Find Me

In God there is no hunger that needs to be filled, only plenteousness that desires to give.

—C. S. Lewis, *The Four Loves*

It is not good for the man to be alone.

—Genesis 2:18

Part of being human, as we have already discovered from the *Catechism*, is that we are able to enter into communion with other people and with God. We aren't meant to live alone or in isolation. God created us in and for relationship and communion. This simple truth is why you want your family to be happy. It's why you want your marriage or your parents' marriage to be peaceful and full of love. It's also why it hurts so much when friends and family die, betray you, leave you, or do something together without telling you about it.

So often we try to deny the pain of being left out or abandoned, but it cuts deeply into who we are as human beings. For those who are incarcerated, one of the worst punishments given out by prison guards is solitary confinement, in which the prisoner is left alone and without any human inter-action for twenty-three hours a day. We need other people, and it is in giving ourselves to others as a gift and receiving others as a gift that we find out what it means to be human.

During my third year of playing Division I college volleyball, I developed a knee injury that required surgery. It was a daunting task just to board an airplane a few days after the operation; and then I had to retrain my leg muscles to function together again efficiently. The athletic trainer who worked with me for months after the surgery won a place deep in my heart for her selfless kindness during that time.

She knew that the physical rehabilitation would be painful, so she accompanied me throughout the entire process. She led me through workouts, helped me get stronger in the weight room, tended to my physical pain in the middle of the night while we were on team road trips, and never complained about all the extra time she had to spend working with me. I truly needed help during that time in my life—I couldn't rehabilitate myself on my own—and she gave me the gift of herself in service, teaching me what it meant to be diligent and consistent. My life is surely better because of that wonderful and generous woman.

Communion and relationship speak to us on the deepest levels. The relationships we have on earth are supposed to reflect the deep love and care that God has for us. The intimacy we experience with one another is a small spark of the intimacy God desires to have with us.

In music and art, we hear and see countless works that celebrate love or mourn the loss of love. Even in the genre of classical music, I can hear the swells and strains of love. Many times, as I listen to the works of Chopin or Rachmaninoff, I sit in stunned silence over the beauty that is pouring into my heart. The harmonies and melodies shine in loving communion with one another. Whether it be expressed through modern music or medieval art, relationship and communion are clearly the language of the heart. So it is natural that when our relationships are happy and fulfilling, we are usually happy and fulfilled. When they are disordered and broken, we often reflect that same unhappiness. In our hearts, we desire love that is authentic and ordered. We desire to be found and embraced by the one we love.

I have a dear friend who has always been an incredible witness to me of maturity and fullness of life. From the very first moment I met him, I sensed grace (which is the very life of God in the human soul) emanating from him. He and his wife and children have a beautiful ministry to teenagers, and they share their love and life with everyone they meet.

This man often tells a story from when his children were very young. He had taken three of them to a park to play hide-and-seek and was counting out loud while the kids found a place to hide. My friend laughs when he tells the story because when it was time for him to seek, his two little boys were hiding in plain view under the jungle gym, his daughter wasn't too far away, and they were all giggling. Playing along with them, my friend pretended not to see the kids and in a roundabout way began his search for them.

As he drew closer and closer to their location, he suddenly jumped in front of them and shouted, "I see you!" His boys took off running so they wouldn't get tagged, but his daughter looked at him, jumped into his arms, and said, "Hold me, Daddy, for a long, long time!" My friend reminisces that while his little girl didn't quite get hide-and-seek, she got the most important lesson of all: that we all want to be sought after, found, and held by the perfect father, who is God.

Jesus speaks to this yearning for union and intimacy when he talks to the crowds about marriage. After speaking about the provision for divorce Moses made in the law, Jesus says to the crowd, "From the beginning, it was not so" (Mt 19:8). These few words reveal something very rich. Pope John Paul II wrote extensively on this discourse from the Gospel of Matthew in his work on the Theology of the Body.[1] The Holy Father beautifully illumines the profound relationship that existed between Adam and Eve in the garden before original sin, before the fall of man.

Before sin entered the world, God's grace suffused his creation. There was no death or disorder, and there was no disharmony between Adam and Eve. There was no lust, no using of one another, no divorce. They were "naked, yet they felt no shame" (Gen 2:25) because each saw the complete beauty and gift of the other. They neither feared losing one another, nor desired to take advantage of one another. In the garden, Adam and Eve knew God and were known by God, and they also knew one another as man and wife in the beautiful marital union.

In this story, we find the first instance of authentic human intimacy, characterized by a harmony that is only possible in the life of grace. True intimacy is found in knowing and being known by the other, and this longing for intimacy is written in the fiber of our hearts, souls, and bodies.

When I was fifteen years old, I really wanted a watch for my birthday. I told my mom, and a few days before my birthday, she took me to the mall. On the way to the store, my mom told me that she had already purchased a watch for me but, after thinking about it, had decided she wanted me to choose the one I liked best. She kept her gift hidden in her purse as she led me to the watch counter to pick out my favorite. I remember looking at all those watches—there must have been over forty different ones. After some time, I selected a style that came in either black or white. I studied both watches and then chose the black one with the mother-of-pearl face.

Happy to have found one I really liked, I looked at my mom, who smiled and then pulled out of her purse the identical watch, which she had purchased the week before. The saleswoman at the counter gasped and then laughed, saying, "Wow, you two really think alike." How delightful it is to be known by someone! And this example is just a pale reflection of how we are known and loved by God our Father.

We call God Father for a reason. By calling him Father, we acknowledge that he is the creator and author of all things, but we also acknowledge being his sons and daughters. This relationship means that we are never alone and that we are not orphans. It means that even if we have earthly parents who are broken and who may hurt us, even through all that, we are never forgotten or unloved by God. God does not cause bad things to happen to us, nor does he delight in suffering and sorrow. And God is not limited by the brokenness in this world: he takes what is dark and torn asunder and transforms it into beauty beyond imagination. God is not made in our image and likeness—we are made in his. We belong to him.

Because we are created by God, we are created with a certain order. God is very orderly! Notice how the sun rises each day and sets each evening. Notice how the seasons always follow one another in the same pattern. Even the human person grows up within a certain order. The child begins very, very small in the womb of the mother and grows in an orderly fashion (rather slowly on a daily basis) into an adult. We never have to wonder how people will biologically grow up. We know that there is an order to creation, there is an order in nature. Our interior life is very similar.

The *Catechism* tells us that human beings are "capable of knowledge, self-possession, and freedom" (*CCC* 357). God gives us all an intellect to know the good, a will to choose the good, and our emotions (passions) to move us toward the good. This order of the human person is very beautiful and very important. When we function properly, it's like a symphony of goodness that brings us true freedom. Freedom, in the fullest sense, isn't doing what we want, when, where, how, and with whom we want. That's more like license. Freedom is being able to identify what is truly good and to then choose the good. To see the awesome beauty of another person and to then choose to honor that beauty rather than lust after it is freedom. To do

what is best for ourselves and others is true freedom. When we live in freedom, we don't have to
hide or run away from God, ourselves, or others.

I wonder how much of my life I have spent playing hide-and-seek with God. In all the ways we are
disordered, we seek to hide from God, ourselves,
and others. Sometimes I think that if people knew
certain things about me, they would run away. Fear
can keep any of us in isolation, not unlike the pris-
oners in solitary confinement. I sometimes fear that
there are parts of me that even God does not love,
and I fear knowing the truth about myself. Perhaps
our culture's aversion to silence comes from a fear
of what we will find or have to face in the silence,
so we keep busy and noisy to hide from God. But
he doesn't get tired of waiting and seeking us out.
And when you and I allow ourselves to be found
by him, he takes us in his arms and holds us to his
heart. Pope Francis remarks:

> God is in every person's life. Even if the
> life of a person has been a disaster, even
> if it is destroyed by vices, drugs, or any-
> thing else—God is in this person's life.
> You can, you must try to seek God in
> every human life. Although the life of a
> person is a land full of thorns and weeds,
> there is always a space in which the good
> seed can grow. You have to trust God.[3]

No matter what has happened in our lives, God stays with us to see us through. There is always hope. He is the Father who never gives up on us and who always sees us as we truly are. He is the Son who loves us so much that he gave his life for us. He is the Holy Spirit who breathes life into us and brings us back from the dead. God isn't fooled by our masks or our attempts to deter him. He seeks communion with us and he seeks to restore us to relationship with himself, ourselves, and others. He longs to touch what is disordered within us so we can live with joy in his love. You and I don't need to live in fear because God goes before us, and he is the Father who never leaves or forsakes us (see Dt 31:6). Let him find you and delight in you.

Prayer: God, please come and find me in the places where I hide from you. Please give me the gift of hope when I feel disappointed, discouraged, and despairing. Give me the courage to be still so I can be found by you. May I be open to your embrace, the embrace that brings communion, healing, and restoration. Amen.

Questions for Deeper Reflection:

Answer as honestly as you can and bring your answers, desires, and fears to God.

- What are the some of the ways God has revealed himself to me as my Father?

- How do I feel about being completely known by God? Are there areas in my life that I want to hide from him, myself, or others?

- Where in my life do I have a lot of hope and expectation? Where in my life do I have a lot of fear and discouragement?

- What are my greatest hopes in relation to God? What do I desire to see happen in my relationship with him?

Chapter 4

Mend My
Broken Heart

---

*The very first tear he made was so deep
that I thought it had gone right into my
heart.*

> —C. S. Lewis, *The Voyage of the Dawn Treader*

*Can a mother forget her infant,
be without tenderness for the child of her
    womb?
Even should she forget,
I will never forget you.
See, upon the palms of my hands I have
    engraved you;
your walls are ever before me.*

> —Isaiah 49:15–16

All children want to know where they came from—
they want to know their story. I was no different.
Around the age of seven, I became very interested
in the baby pictures of me that my mom had pasted
into a huge scrapbook chronicling our life as a family. There were pictures of my parents' first house,
fishing and skiing trips, and even one of my brother

tying himself to the seesaw in the backyard. I spent many hours looking at all those pictures, and after a while I noticed something was missing. One day when my parents and I were riding in the car on a road trip, I took advantage of the long journey to finally ask my mom the question that had been troubling me. "Mom," I asked, "how come there aren't any pictures of you pregnant with me?"

There was a long silence between my parents. The answer my mom eventually gave me changed my entire life and my view of the world. "Honey," she began in a gentle and delicate voice, "your dad and I wanted to have children very much, but we could not. So we contacted a group of people who help parents adopt children. Your birth mother and birth father were very young when they had you. They loved you very much and wanted to keep you, but they knew they were too young. They wanted what was best for you, so they gave you up for adoption, and we got to adopt you."

It's hard to put into words exactly what went on in my heart as a little girl at that moment. How do you comprehend that your origin and entire existence are different from what you thought? Out of fear that people would treat me differently, my parents urged me to keep the story of my adoption to myself. Part of my heart went numb that day. The truth felt like a big, dark secret that needed to be contained and hidden. Who was I, anyway?

I have thought about that moment many times since becoming an adult. My mother and I have had several discussions about that conversation in the car, about my story, and about my origins. I have often wondered if God knew what he was doing on that day when two seventeen-year-old kids came together and then apart after conceiving me. What did he think of the turmoil that surely ensued when my birth mother realized she was pregnant? Abortion was legal in America at that time—did that option play upon her mind? What does that say about me? The question of who I really am is one that only human beings can have, and it goes far beyond this earth to touch the face of eternity. The truth is that I am not an "unplanned pregnancy." I am a human being.

From God's perspective, there is no such thing as an "unplanned pregnancy." No one is a mistake or an accident to God. It took a very long time and much prayer, counseling, and healing for this truth to permeate my heart and my mind. I thought for years that since my biological parents most likely did not intend to conceive me and did not want to raise me, I was not meant to be here on earth. It was very easy to feel like a product of an unintended circumstance rather than the intentional creation of divine destiny. The deep pain of having been rejected by my biological parents etched a noticeable scar on my life. Due to this wound of abandonment, I struggled with feeling precious or delighted in by the loved ones around me.

Why would God allow something like this to happen? The fullness of the situation is a mystery this side of heaven. God honors the biological nature he has given to humanity; he blesses the union of man and woman even if they are unaware of the consequences of that union. From the very beginning of creation, God reveals his delight in life. In the Garden of Eden, his first command is one of blessing and goodness. "God blessed [Adam and Eve] and God said to them: Be fertile and multiply; fill the earth and subdue it. Have dominion over the fish of the sea, the birds of the air, and all the living things that crawl on the earth" (Gen 1:28). God has no evil or ill desires toward us; he wishes us to be fruitful, happy, and strong. But something went horribly awry.

You and I know that the world we live in is very broken. It was broken in the past, and it is broken now. We see countries at war, marriages dissolving, and bitter hatred within families and nations. The Centers for Disease Control and Prevention states that despite the prevalence of sex education by government organizations and an increased use in contraception, young people aged fifteen to twenty-four still acquire half of all new cases of sexually transmitted diseases every year.[1] Since the legalization of abortion by *Roe v. Wade* in 1973, Americans have legally aborted more than fifty-five million children.[2] Drug use is rampant in our country, and the rise of atheistic and socialist movements among Americans is troubling. We can look out into the world, into our own families, and even into our own hearts, and see brokenness and sorrow. When we experience it, we cry out for a better world. You and I weren't made for sin and sorrow because "from the beginning, it was not so."

We don't have time to sketch out the entire fall of man here, but we do have to understand that humanity was created in and for complete goodness and love but then chose another path. Sometimes people make jokes about Eve eating an apple or seem to think that sin (translated from a Greek archery term that literally means "to miss the mark") is something medieval and that we as a race have "progressed" beyond such archaic thinking. Nothing could be further from the truth. We encounter sin all around us every day. As Catholics, we call the fundamental rupture between Adam, Eve, and God *original sin*. Pope John Paul II gives one of the best and most concise explanations of original sin in his popular book *Crossing the Threshold of Hope*: "This is truly the key for interpreting reality. . . . Original sin attempts, then, to abolish fatherhood."[3] In its essence, original sin attacks the very fatherhood of God.

In the third chapter of the book of Genesis, we find the story of Satan encountering Eve and saying something along the lines of, "You think God is really your loving Father? You think he truly loves you and wants what is best for you? He doesn't. He wants to dominate you and keep you subservient and powerless. If you want freedom and if you want to be happy, you had better reach out and take what God has forbidden because you won't find freedom and happiness any other way."[4] In the moment that follows, in all its mystery, Eve grasps for illusory happiness, urging her husband to do so as well, and they rupture their relationship with God the Father. Instead of living in trust, love, and freedom, they end up living in fear, shame, and blame.

The lie that Satan seeks to implant in our hearts is that we are orphans; that we are fatherless and all alone. Does this sound familiar to you? Do you hear this lie anywhere in your own heart? We can see this thought and its consequences everywhere throughout history and to this present day. In our rejection of God as Father and our subsequent fall from grace, we are shattered and disordered. Our intellect is at war with our will, and our will is at war with our passions and emotions. We are dis-integrated, and we know this situation all too well. Sin has consequences, and we often find ourselves trying to escape the consequences or blaming God and others for our problems.

When we reject God, to whom we belong and in whose image and likeness we are made, we reject what it means to be truly human. We become blind, and in our blindness we disregard and discard the work of his hands. Rather than live in peace as children of God Most High, we try to become our own gods, deciding what is good and what is evil, and the results are disastrous.

I certainly don't think my birth parents knew what they were in for when they came together the day I was conceived. Did they know that moment would affect them and so many others for the rest of their lives? I doubt it. Even though they felt that adoption was the best possible choice they could make for me, I still bear the scars and fears of rejection and abandonment. My life will always be marked by a choice that was made by other people. We are all marked by similar things. Choices have consequences, but I am so grateful that my biological mother chose life for me even though it most likely came at a very high cost to her personally.

What we do with our bodies matters. As women, we are told the lie by society that we can do whatever we want with our bodies, that it's no one else's business. Unfortunately, if a woman gets pregnant, she is often told that the child in her womb is merely a "choice," that she can "terminate the pregnancy" if she wants to. I speak very reverently here to all those men and women whose lives have been touched by such a tremendously sad and conflicting decision, such a deep sorrow.

Abortion always brings death to the child, a unique child who can never be recreated. Abortion always wounds the mother and the father, for killing a person for any reason must affect us. Abortion actually affects everybody on the face of the earth. Because of abortion, we are missing friends and relatives. We are missing leaders, thinkers, and spouses; we are missing countless children that *those* children would have had. We are missing entire generations of human beings, and the loss is staggering.[5] Choices have consequences.

In our hearts, we all long for a better way. We long for safety, refuge, and belonging. We long for goodness, love, and peace. Because of God and his love for us, there is always hope for redemption, no matter what we have done or what has been done to us. No matter where you find yourself at this moment, God is seeking you and desiring to heal you and restore you. Out of the darkness, even sorrow such as this, can come great light.

As the questions of my origin and birth came more frequently to my heart as an adult, I started speaking about them to trusted friends and began to research the particular joys and struggles of those who are adopted. When I saw the adoption papers and the physical description of my birth parents,

I wept. When I read the account of my stay as a newborn in a temporary foster home, I sorrowed for the infant who was in many ways an orphan. Sitting with the pain of those deprivations was not easy, and it is still difficult at times. I cried out to God many times as I came up against the darkness of uncontrollable fear and anxiety and a broken, abandoned heart. The journey of honesty about pain while waiting for healing with an open heart isn't easy, but it's worth it. We don't have to live with the darkness that stalks the corners of our hearts and minds and cast shadows upon the light of joy. You and I have a good Father who loves us with a tremendous love and who has the power to make crooked ways straight.

Prayer: Father, thank you for never giving up on me. Even in my bitterness and anger, you love me. In my pain, shame, and sorrow, you love me. You aren't dismayed by my brokenness nor are you turned away by my messiness. You just love me and you seek to heal me. Father, I pray for those with broken hearts. I pray for those who have secrets of rejection and abandonment. I pray for your tender and gentle light to dawn in my heart. Please come and be with me right where I am. Amen.

Questions for Deeper Reflection:

Answer as honestly as you can and bring your answers, desires, and fears to God.

- What is the story of my conception and birth? Were my parents happy about my arrival or was there sorrow or sickness in the family?

- How do I see the sickness of sin affecting my life right now? Do I have particular sins or areas in which I struggle deeply?

- Are there any secrets in my life that I am keeping?

- What would I like God to do for me at this moment?

Chapter 5

Untangle My Secrets

Tell me your sorrows.

> —C. S. Lewis, *The Horse and His Boy*

*Because I kept silent, my bones wasted
    away;
I groaned all day long.
For day and night your hand was heavy
    upon me;
my strength withered as in dry summer
    heat.
Then I declared my sin to you;
my guilt I did not hide.
I said, "I confess my transgression to the
    Lord,"
and you took away the guilt of my sin.*

> —Psalm 32:3–5

No one wants to be an addict. No one says, "I want to be addicted and unhappy when I grow up!" Yet so many people find themselves in that situation today. In reality, all of us are addicted to something, dependent to the point that it is beyond our control. We all use and grasp at things that we think will fill the aching emptiness within us. We try to fill the emptiness with food or work or relationships; we try to quell the pain with alcohol, drugs, shopping, or sex. We all, indeed, "groan within ourselves as we wait for adoption, the redemption of our bodies" (Rom 8:23). We are all looking for redemption, and we long for the time when "[God] will wipe every tear from [our] eyes, and there shall be no more death or mourning, wailing or pain, [for] the old order has passed away" (Rv 21:4). The exterior addiction is often a symptom of a deeper sorrow.

My career in addiction started early. It was well before my twenty-first birthday when I first drank alcohol to excess. In fact, by the time I was twenty-one, I was already an alcoholic. Oh, not the kind you find living under a bridge clutching a bottle wrapped in a brown paper bag. In fact, it was that stereotype of the alcoholic that kept me in denial for a long time. "Well," I told myself, "I don't drink every day, and I don't miss school or work or anything because of drinking, and I don't live under a bridge. There's no way I'm an alcoholic." Yet within my heart, I knew the truth about myself, that I was a problem drinker. I just didn't have the strength to admit it. When something that you want to deny keeps poking you in the heart, it's a good idea to take a look at it.

What I have learned since is that "social" drinkers don't begin drinking at twelve years of age. It isn't "normal" to drink to excess nearly every single

time one picks up a drink. "Normal" drinkers don't
have blackouts on a fairly regular basis. They also
don't wake up in the morning with deep regrets,
plan when they can drink again, or promise themselves they will never drink that much again, only
to fall into the same pattern over and over. These
were realities I knew only too well. This is a cycle of
addiction, no matter what form the addiction may
take. I promised myself I would stop. I would cry
out to God for help, and yet the pattern continued.
What was the problem? Why couldn't I get my
act together? The situation was confounding and
soul-wrenching, and I felt so much shame about
myself and my struggles.

And so the questions came: Was I a bad person?
Was I evil? No and no. I was just sick on many levels and unable to heal or fix myself. It's true on a
certain level that I did want to stop drinking, but I
wasn't ready to face the deeper pain that drove my
addiction. Addictions are usually a feeble attempt to
escape emotional pain in our lives. We learn disordered ways of running from and dealing with pain,
but it still remains.

As I mentioned earlier, we long for beauty and
freedom; we yearn for redemption. This struggle we
have with sin—our own and the sins of others—was
never meant to be "from the beginning." Life can
be very painful on this side of Eden, and the secrets

we keep have the ability to keep us in darkness and bondage.

Psychologists report that one in four girls and one in six boys will be sexually abused by the time they are eighteen.[1] The severity of the abuse varies but all of it deeply wounds the victim and leaves life-long scars and struggles. Many adults bear these wounds and have spoken of the abuse to no one. Sexual abuse can lead the victim to shame, guilt, depression, self-hatred, substance abuse, promiscuity, and other distress. Even if silently behind a mask of people-pleasing and tentativeness, the victim cries out for healing, restoration, and a release from the pain.

I should know. It happened to me.

How do children deal with sexual abuse? How do they make sense of the invasion and violation of their body, mind, and soul? How do they integrate the conflicting feelings and thoughts? Most often they don't without some sort of help. As with the inner knowledge I had of my problem drinking, so I always knew on a deeper level of the abuse I suffered as a child. I didn't tell anyone what happened during those instances of violation, and I couldn't admit it to myself on a conscious level, but underneath, I knew. I remembered, and I hurt. In that hurt, I hurt myself and others.

My relationship with my parents became strained as I kept more and more secrets from them and acted out in secret. I began rebelling against my mother in particular by lying to her and being disrespectful of her, refusing to share the deepest parts of myself with her. I did not tell either of my parents what had happened to me, and that secret created a rift between us and produced a lot of unexpressed anger and resentment within me that would later manifest for me as clinical depression. The pain and darkness became like an infectious disease that festered within.

I remember sitting by the window one day as a girl after a certain instance of the abuse. I had been taken advantage of for the abuser's gratification and then cast aside when it was over. I felt completely emptied by the abuse and subsequent disorder that shattered my interior life and innocence.

As I sat there and stared at my socks, I was heartbroken and confused, feeling completely stripped of anything good, true, or beautiful. After the abuse, something within me died, or at least fell into a deep sleep. I realize now that it was hope and beauty that died within my little-girl heart that day. No one saw what had happened to me, and no one came to rescue me.

From those moments on, I hated my abuser. I began to hate myself and I thought God hated me, too. The authors of the book *Helping Victims of Sexual Abuse* write, "Distortions about God became an integral part of the human condition in the Garden of Eden. Adam and Eve became afraid and hid from God after their first image of God had become distorted because of sin. God suddenly looked 'different' to them from their fallen state."[2]

God looked very different to me through the broken lens of abuse. How could he let this happen? Did he not care about me? Why didn't he protect me? I was angry with God, full of deep resentment, and I just wanted the pain to stop. Although people have varied responses to abuse, my response was perfectionism, alcohol addiction, using men and allowing them to use me, buried anger and resentment that produced chronic depression, and shame.

A person who is abused or taken advantage of loses the joy of being some *one* to love and be loved (beloved), entering instead into the barren territory of being some *thing* that is used and then discarded when the "pleasure" has passed. It is truly a cosmic rupture to be used rather than loved. In the depths of our DNA, we are meant for love. We are made by, for, and in Love; and many of our happiest memories come from an experience of being loved and delighted in. These glimpses of the bliss of true love foreshadow an eternal reality. The *Catechism* reveals that "God is love and in himself he lives a mystery of personal loving communion. Creating the human race in his own image, God inscribed in the humanity of man and woman the *vocation*, and thus the capacity and responsibility, *of love* and communion" (*CCC* 2331). We are all called to love and communion. This ordering of the self through the grace and healing of Jesus is what we might call *purity*.

Society fills our heads and our hearts with the message that we can use one another with "no strings attached," no consequences. The mainstream media mock any sort of chaste (I am defining chastity as rightly ordered love) desires and spurn the very notion of purity as an archaic, guilt-ridden, right-wing Christian imposition. I read a book not too long ago in which the premise rested entirely on the idea that the desire for purity of heart and body is really a myth perpetuated by oppressive religious extremists.

Now, there are some religious groups that misunderstand what purity really is and mistakenly undervalue the beauty of sexuality and the body. These groups therefore present sexuality in a negative light, but that doesn't mean that the desire for sexual purity is an oppressive myth. As a matter of fact, we desire purity in all other aspects of our life. We want clean water and clean clothes, we want our trash picked up every Thursday morning, and we don't like smokers sitting next to us on an airplane flight or in a restaurant. We want pure things. To claim that we don't really desire purity and integration in our hearts and bodies makes no sense.

We may settle for that kind of rationale because we are hurting and think that purity—the healing and restoration of authentic love—is beyond our reach or effort, but this doesn't negate the continual longing of our hearts to love and be loved, rather than use and be used.

If using people were the path to happiness, our world would be a complete utopia. However, as many people have realized, we have more sex but less love than ever. We are made for more than this. We are made for more than using one another for our personal pleasure. We are made for more than brokenness and addiction. The pain we face in our lives may seem insurmountable, but there is always hope. God has not abandoned us. He sees and knows everything, and within the painful mysteries of our life that Satan uses to try to destroy us, God the Warrior fights for our redemption and healing.

It was many years before I earnestly told another person what had happened to me as a child. Shame compounds shame, and I fought very hard to hide behind the mask of perfectionism. I thought that if I could get my exterior to look perfect enough, no one would see the darkness and self-hatred I felt within. The idea of purity pierced my heart as something I had lost and could never regain. It seemed like a nice virtue for other people, but when I looked at my life—what had happened to me and what I had done—I didn't think it was something that would ever be reasonable for me. It was for "good girls" who had never made mistakes, and I wasn't a good girl. I kept everyone at a distance and harbored a deep suspicion of God, affection, love, and men.

This sort of unkindness toward and judgment of others is usually more of a reflection of our own hearts than a realistic depiction of the other person. The betrayal of abuse goes very deep, and it's only in the slow restoration of all that is crushed and distorted in the victim's heart that the authentic beauty of that person begins to shine again.

The psalmist expressed so powerfully this kind of desolation in Psalm 32:3: *"Because I kept silent, my bones wasted away, I groaned all day long."*

I know this feeling, having kept my secrets until "my frame was wasted." It was only after I entered religious life that I uttered a word of the immense shame that I was carrying. Telling my secrets to someone trustworthy and loving wasn't easy, and it probably never will be, but it's worth it. It does get better. Even as I write this, I smile. It does get better. Healing and freedom are real when we allow Christ to purify our hearts of those scars we tried to hide for so long, in vain. In the process, we may come to realize that purity is not a prize to be won, but a beautiful and sacred gift to be received and cherished.

In his book *Addiction and Grace*, Gerald May writes that "Addiction may oppress our desire, erode our wills, confound our motivations, and contaminate our judgment, but its bondage is never absolute."[3] Even in the throes of our deepest addictions and pain, the human spirit continually rises for resurrection. While we are on this earth, there is always hope for restoration and resurrection.

I don't know what you are facing within your heart at this moment. Maybe you have been sexually abused or assaulted and you haven't told anyone. Maybe you struggle with cutting yourself, same-sex attraction, pornography, or masturbation. Perhaps you struggle with perfectionism, fear, depression, mental illness, or anger. Maybe you have done everything "right" in your life and yet you still feel empty. Whatever it is that you are facing, God wants to face it with you. We will talk about recovery in a later chapter; what I would like to emphasize to you now is that Jesus meets you where you are. You don't have to spend the rest of your life hiding deep secrets. You don't have to spend the rest of your life hurting from the pain of the past. Christ's healing is real, and there is always hope. Sin, pain, and death do not have the last word. The first and last Word is Jesus Christ.

Prayer: Jesus, please reveal your tender and strong heart to me. Please come and be with me as I explore the painful areas of my heart. May I know your love for me and your desire to set me free. May your Mother Mary gently hold me and continuously lead me closer to you. Amen.

Questions for Deeper Reflection:

Answer as honestly as you can and bring your answers, desires, and fears to God.

- Are there things I have done or that have been done to me that I have never told anyone about?

- What might be some areas of addiction that I turn to in order to diminish pain within my heart or life?

- Do I have serious addictions that are destructive to me or my family?

- How do I understand purity? Do I see it as something negative or unreasonable? Do I recognize and sense my desire for true purity and redemption? How do I see this manifested in my heart and relationships?

- Do I feel abandoned by God or am I angry at him because of the pain in my life? Write him a letter or verbalize your grief. He can take your pain and sorrow; he isn't deterred by it.

Chapter 6

Wipe Away My Tears

*"This," said Reepicheep, "is where I go on
alone."*

—C. S. Lewis, *The Voyage of the Dawn Treader*

*Do not let the flood waters overwhelm me,
nor the deep swallow me,
nor the pit close its mouth over me.*

—Psalm 69:16

When the phone rings late at night, it never seems
to be good news. We all fear that phone call, the
phone call that brings unbearable news. I was living
in Rome as a novice when mine came. I was in my
room and all was quiet when I heard the phone ring
downstairs. Something about the call struck fear in
my heart—who could it be?

My superior answered the phone, and after a
time of quiet the thought left my mind. However,
twenty minutes later, she knocked on my door.
As she told me that my mom was on the phone, I
could see the glint of tears in her eyes illumined by
the streetlight shining through the window. With a
sickening fear in the pit of my stomach, I picked up
the phone to receive whatever sorrow was about to
befall me.

Most of us don't grow up thinking about death. Maybe we have a grandfather or a great-aunt who passes away when we are children, but for many people death doesn't hit home until we grow older. We spend our teenage years thinking we are invincible and that this thing called death surely will not come to us or those we love. We feel sorry when we hear stories about young children who pass away or other young people who die in tragic accidents. We feel sorry, and then we move on with our lives. But death does catch up with us. Death comes to those we love, and it touches us to the core of our being. Death leaves a lot of questions and stirs up a million more.

The news my mom told me on the phone that night was sorrowful indeed. As I pressed the receiver to my ear, my mother's tearful voice poured out the story that my seemingly healthy father had just been diagnosed with pancreatic cancer and that it was terminal. Having just seen my dad over the summer, I struggled to fathom what my mother was telling me. My vitamin-obsessed parents were so healthy that they didn't even have a regular doctor. Heck, my dad even went to work the day he had ulcer surgery many years earlier. My mom and dad were presently at one of our S.O.L.T. missions doing volunteer construction work. They were happy and healthy and living a full life. They were good people. How was this happening to us?

The question of suffering, why bad things happen to good people, has plagued humanity, generation after generation. Many different philosophies try to explain this paradox. Some people say that suffering is God's fault. Others say that suffering is a result of our own desires and attachments to things. Most of us try to avoid suffering outright. We live in a society that runs from suffering at any cost and pretends it doesn't exist. Yet it still remains. This struggle with suffering speaks to the fact that somehow we know we are not meant to suffer, that something is inherently wrong in our reality.

And it's true—something is very wrong. Suffering and death are a cosmic tragedy. The original sin we talked about earlier doesn't just affect how we relate to God, to ourselves, and to others; it has altered every facet of our existence, including allowing the inevitability of death.

The *Catechism* explains that "even though man's nature is mortal, God had destined him not to die. Death was therefore contrary to the plans of God the Creator and entered the world as a consequence of sin" (*CCC* 1008). God didn't create death. God isn't sadistic: he does not inflict sorrow or evil, and he doesn't wish to see people suffer. A friend of mine likes to say, "God is all good. He cannot give what he doesn't have. He cannot give evil or darkness." So often we think it is God who crushes us in our sorrow. Under the weight of suffering, whatever suffering it may be, we cry out in our agony.

Time seemed to stand still as we stood near my father's bed in the hospital. Our world as a little family had completely shattered; everything seemed to have stopped in the midst of this horrible reality that was upon us. We tried to defy the odds. My dad tried chemotherapy and when that didn't work, he tried vitamins and herbs. Holy priests prayed over him, and loving friends and family prayed for him. We did everything we could think of to bring about his healing.

As my dad's condition deteriorated, I clung to the hope that somehow God would heal him and let him stay here on earth with us. It broke my heart to see his body deteriorate knowing that we were all helpless to stop it. I couldn't believe that cancer was taking the life of such a noble and good man, a man we still needed here on earth. My family wasn't ready to say goodbye to my father—it was too soon and too tragic.

One of the most powerful movies ever made is Mel Gibson's *The Passion of the Christ*. It renders people speechless and evokes deep movements of the heart and mind when watched attentively. In fact, it's such a challenge to watch the entire movie that it's usually shown only in churches or at events during Lent and Holy Week. I've never heard anyone say,

"Hey, what are you doing Saturday night? Wanna watch *The Passion*?" You have to prepare mentally to watch the realistic and personal depiction of Jesus willingly suffering and dying for us. I saw the film in the theater and have watched it several times since. Some of the most moving scenes for me are those depicting the beautiful relationship between Jesus and Mary.

The first time I saw the movie, I think nearly every woman in the theater wept during the scene in which Mary watches Jesus fall down under the weight of his cross. The movie shows that event evoking in Mary a memory from Jesus' childhood when he fell down and she rushed to her little boy to embrace him and comfort him. This time, though, she couldn't pick him up, kiss his wounds, and make the pain go away. She was, in a very real sense, powerless to stop the evil. She had to watch her son suffer cruel torture and a shameful death. I am sure it was too soon and too tragic for Mary, the human mother. She knew that "and you yourself a sword will pierce" (Lk 2:35), but suffering always has a way of shaking us.

In looking at her experience, though, we see a profound beauty and power in her response to suffering. Mary didn't run away. She didn't seek revenge and she didn't cower in fear. She walked with her son to the very end; she accompanied him in his passion and death. Despite her own pain, she gave herself entirely to the one who was suffering, uniting her heart to his. She did not let Jesus walk alone. This is the beautiful fierceness of a woman's heart. She walks boldly into the darkness to bring her grace-filled light.

For my family and me, our worst fear on earth did come to pass. My father fell into a coma as his body began to swell from massive fluid retention. A stream of visitors came to the hospital to pray for him, bless him, and console us. In the end, his passing was very quiet. He was released from the ICU to a private room, where my mother and I stayed by his side as his breathing revealed his passage from this life. We fell asleep only to be awakened suddenly by something unknown.

We began to pray the Rosary for him and then stood on either side of his bed. As we finished the prayers and began a final plea to Mary, the Mother of Jesus who knows and loves her son and who suffered with him for all of us, my father took three final breaths. After he exhaled for the last time, the room became utterly silent and was filled with an incredible peace. In one of the most sorrowful situations I have ever experienced, the beauty of God filled that room and our hearts. The shock, loss, and grief were real but so were the peace, comfort, and beauty.

The *Catechism* again: "In death, God calls man to himself. Therefore the Christian can experience a desire for death like St. Paul's: 'My desire is to depart and be with Christ.' He can transform his own death into an act of obedience and love towards the Father, after the example of Christ" (*CCC* 1011). In other words, we do not die alone nor do we go into a formless void. In death, the faithful enter into the abundant life with Christ. Everything flows out of Christ and goes back into him. Jesus says of himself, "I am the Alpha and the Omega, the first and the last, the beginning and the end" (Rv 22:13). Nothing happens to us without the knowledge of God. Jesus knew my dad was suffering, and he knew that my family and all who knew my father were suffering. Jesus was there with my father as he left this earth and entered into eternal life. He was with us, as well. We are all made for life and we will live forever, whether with God or without him.

J. R. R. Tolkien's great trilogy *The Lord of the Rings* compellingly dramatizes the human experience, teaching many important lessons. In the movie version of the first volume, *The Fellowship of the Ring*, Gandalf and Frodo have a profound conversation about the nature of evil, pity, and destiny. They are lost in the Mines of Moria. Frodo exclaims, "I wish the Ring had never come to me. I wish none of this had happened."

Gandalf responds, "So do all who live to see such times, but that is not for them to decide. All we have to decide is what to do with the time that is given to us."

Who among us could not say the very same thing as Frodo when facing deep suffering? The burden that Frodo willingly accepted was far heavier than he could have imagined. It nearly cost him his life. It took everyone in the Fellowship to help Frodo to Mount Doom; the journey would not have succeeded without the cooperation of all. Yet even at the end of the journey, it is suffering that saves him. As Frodo is about to turn in on himself and keep the One Ring for himself rather than destroy it in the fire, suffering intervenes and saves him and all Middle Earth.

One of the enigmatic things about suffering is that it can lead us out of ourselves into communion with others. Suffering can soften our hearts to those who mourn, those who sorrow, those who hunger and thirst. It is no coincidence that the author of Hebrews writes, "For we do not have a high priest who is unable to sympathize with our weaknesses, but one who has similarly been tested in every way, yet without sin" (Heb 4:15). Jesus does not come as one who scorns, admonishes, and punishes. He comes as one who is poor, humble, and suffering. The power of his humility shatters the bonds of darkness and death: it shatters the darkness of our hearts and minds, and it shatters the separation of death. In the midst of things we wish would never happen, Jesus shows up and redeems our hearts.

Even though my dad passed away more than ten years ago now, I still miss him. Sometimes when I visit my mom, I still half expect my dad to come downstairs in the morning with a cup of coffee. My dad still lives, just not here on earth. Losing a loved one is not something you ever get over; our loved ones are precious, irreplaceable gifts from God. The pain of loss is deep and we bear part of it for the rest of our lives, but as we entrust our loved ones to the mercy of God, they become treasures in our hearts for whom we give thanks. We thank God for creating such wonderful people. We pray for them and ask them to pray for us.

Prayer: Jesus, thank you for the blessing of my loved ones. Thank you for giving me such beautiful people. I ask your special blessing and protection upon them now. Please especially care for those who have died. Have mercy upon them and bring them to see the light of your face. Heal all those who grieve, and give us strength. Amen.

Questions for Deeper Reflection:

Answer as honestly as you can and bring your answers, desires, and fears to God.

- Have I lost a loved one in my life? Have I ever journaled the story? What were my feelings? What is it like now?

- What were my thoughts and feelings about the movie *The Passion of the Christ*? Were there particular scenes that touched me? Why?

- What are my thoughts about death? What does the Catholic Church teach about death? What does Jesus teach about death?

- Can I see any blessings that have been revealed even through the death of a loved one?

Chapter 7

Heal My Wounds

"Who are you?" asked Shasta. "Myself," said the Voice, very deep and low so that the earth shook.

—C. S. Lewis, *The Horse and His Boy*

I am who I am.

—Exodus 3:14

Many of us have had difficult experiences of trying to belong, and remembering how we have seemingly searched and failed or have been rejected even by our family and friends brings deep pain. The pain is a sign that we are made for communion, for so much more than the brokenness we find on this earth. God knows the pain in your heart, and he is not indifferent to it. Whether you have been rejected by your family, been mocked by people at school or work, or have given your heart to someone only to have it shattered and stripped, you are not alone in that sorrow and pain.

In his very nature, God is tender, caring, and healing, and we receive those beautiful characteristics from his heart. God does not abandon his sons and daughters, and we are *all* his sons and daughters. This is the lesson Jesus came to reveal in a profound way. He was so secure in his belonging to God that he could suffer and die for us. Jesus had no identity crisis. The power of his life of belonging to the Father changed the entire course of our destiny; sin and death are destroyed, and healing and life gush forth. Jesus invites us into this abundant life, available to all who want it.

As you have read, my life certainly hasn't been free from pain or sorrow. I bear deep scars from various events in my life and have sought much healing over the years from the sacraments, spiritual direction, twelve-step groups, various types of counseling, books and workbooks, and inner healing prayer as well. Much of this healing has centered on the healing of identity, of who I really am as a daughter of the Father. For when we have wounds of abandonment and rejection, the Evil One uses them as a conduit to whisper the lies that no one loves us and no one will be there for us or care for us. When these wounds go unhealed, our lives become dysfunctional. When these wounds are healed, we can live the abundant life to which Jesus invites us.

Inner healing prayer has been a very powerful instrument of healing in my life. This practice, which is facilitated by an experienced and mature Christian, helps the recipient to find God in the painful memories. It is not make-believe or pretend prayer, since God is indeed everywhere at all times. Inner healing prayer brings that reality to the fore-front and allows the recipient to experience the deep emotion of the memory in a safe environment. Some of my biggest breakthroughs in healing have come from these prayer sessions. I am forever grateful to the authentic ministers of this type of prayer. I have included some references on inner healing at the back of the book in the Additional Resources section.

At one point in my life, many years after enter-ing religious life, I was plagued with anguishing anxiety and crippling fear. It was hard for me to eat or to carry on coherent conversations. I had never suffered panic attacks before, so I was convinced during this time that I was about to lose my mind. I was afraid when I was alone and when I was in a crowd. It felt like an annihilation of darkness was closing its mouth upon me, and I couldn't escape the terror day or night. It was a tremendously try-ing time in my life and I wouldn't wish it upon anyone.

Providentially, God had placed people in my life who were very experienced in dealing with this kind of trauma, and they came to my aid, particu-larly through inner healing prayer. It was in these prayer sessions that the deep anguish I had been trying to stuff down for many years finally arose in my heart. I finally touched the pain of being

abandoned by my biological parents and the hatred
I had toward my abuser, as well as the self-hatred
and shame that had kept me bound for years.

After one particularly powerful prayer ses-
sion in which deliverance took place deep within
my heart, I immediately recalled a certain gospel
story, but in a new way. Sometimes we treat stories
in the gospels as fairy tales or mere relics from a
time far away in the past. We hear the stories Sunday after Sunday and can tune out as the familiar words greet our ears. They don't seem to have
any relevance to our daily life nor do they seem to
be efficacious in changing our hearts. But I would
like you to try something different. I want to share
this gospel story with you, and I invite you to see
yourself in the story. As the story unfolds, find a
place within it and ask Jesus to reveal his heart
to you wherever you find yourself. If you need to
stop during the story and just listen, ponder, or
pray, then do so! Jesus is always speaking to your
heart. Go and get your Bible and spend some time
in this story.

The Gospel of Mark recounts an incredible story
of healing in what seems like an impossible situation (Mk 5:1–20). Jesus begins his ministry to people
other than Jews as he sets off to the "other side of
the sea." When he and his disciples pull their boat
onto shore, they are immediately confronted with

an unpleasant situation: a possessed man comes out from among the tombs to meet them.

This isn't just a man who is bothered now and again by harassing thoughts or spirits; he is completely possessed by a "legion" of spirits. He is so out of control that he lives among the dead in the cemetery. He is naked (which in this area is a sign of having lost his dignity), he is crying out, and he is alone (isolated with no one to love or love him). No one wants to be around this broken and possessed man. Imagine the frustration of his family and friends. No one can do anything with him—he can't even be restrained because he keeps breaking the chains other people use to subdue him. The man is so incredibly broken that he bruises himself with stones as he cries out among the tombs.

Find a place for yourself in this story. Where you do feel drawn to ponder more deeply? Are you one of the disciples, perhaps filled with fear at this horrible and off-putting sight? Do you see yourself at all in the broken and sick man? Do you feel compassion or repulsion?

I see myself in several places. I see the unpleasantness of the sickness of evil and wounds and feel sorrow for the man, but I also see myself wanting to get as far away as possible from him, not wanting to become "unclean" from getting too near him. I also see myself in the sick man. I see parts of myself living among the dead where hope is gone and a

mournful wail of abandonment and despair issues
forth from my heart. I see the self-hatred of the broken parts of my life where I bruise myself with the
stones of sin, condemnation, and self-rejection. And
I feel the discouragement of the sick and possessed
man who may have hoped for healing and transformation, only to be disappointed time and time
again.

Almost in spite of himself, the sick man, seeing
Jesus in the distance, runs to him and falls pros-
trate on the ground in front of him. "What have
you to do with me, Jesus, Son of the Most High
God?" the man cries out (Mk 5:7). Evil knows the
time is short—the spirits are about to be cast out
of this man and they plead for mercy. The heart of
Christ is moved for this sick and broken son of God.
Jesus doesn't offer the man platitudes or shrug his
shoulders and commiserate over the darkness of
the situation. Jesus, completely unafraid and undis-
turbed, casts the evil spirits out of this man, restoring his dignity and sanity. Having seen Jesus cast
the spirits into their swine nearby, the swineherders
run to the town and tell everyone what happened
(news has always traveled fast!), and the people
of the town rush out to the countryside to see this
strange event.

As they draw near, they see Jesus and "they
[catch] sight of the man who had been possessed by
Legion, sitting there clothed and in his right mind"

(Mk 5:15). Mary Healy, in her commentary on the Gospel of Mark, writes that the words "sitting" and "clothed" denote a restoration of this man's peace and dignity. She observes that they are the same words used to describe the young man who is found in Jesus' tomb after his Resurrection (Mk 16:5).[1] Tombs that once contained death now bring life. Seeing the impossible restoration of this sick and broken man, the people in the story are afraid. In their fear, they ask Jesus to leave the area. I wonder how often we do the same thing. In our fear of what God has done or might do, we usher him out of our hearts so we can once again have control of the countryside.

One man, however, doesn't want Jesus to leave. The formerly possessed and sick man pleads to stay with Jesus. Again, Jesus' response is unexpected. Rather than take the man into the boat with him, Jesus tells him to do something very important: "Go home to your family and announce to them all that the Lord in his pity has done for you" (Mk 5:19).

Many times, the most difficult mission assignment we will ever have is the one to our own families. Imagine this man, who had been so broken and unlovely, going home to his family to tell them all the marvelous things that God had done for him. Would they scoff at him and say he was still crazy? Would they mock him and throw his past

brokenness back in his face, saying he had no right
to preach to them after being so broken himself? Or
would they open their hearts and receive this son
who was lost and now is found?

The man didn't neglect his new missionary
assignment. Mark writes, "The man went off and
began to proclaim in the Decapolis what Jesus had
done for him; and all were amazed" (Mk 5:20).
Healy reflects, "The message he had to offer would
have been very simple: 'See the scars? I was the guy
who cut myself and howled at night. I don't do it
anymore!'"[2] So often, the healing of the deepest
brokenness produces the most powerful light. This
man is now on a mission proclaiming the authentic and visible love of God. Do we have the same
courage? Do we proclaim the greatness of God's
mercy on us?

It's beautiful how God always sees the true person, the heart. In this story, the exterior ugliness of
the possessed man is very obvious but it doesn't
stop Jesus from seeing him for who he truly is and
restoring the man's dignity and life. As God comes
for my heart time and time again, he is not deterred
by the ugliness of sin within me and all the walls
I put between us. Jesus continually searches and
seeks for my heart in every situation in my life.
Nothing happens that is beyond his knowledge,
power, or vision.

Pondering again those inner healing prayer sessions, I realize that for most of my life I felt both God the Father and my own biological father (whom I'd never met) had abandoned me. Those lifelong wounds, in addition to the wounds of abuse, had caused me much pain and sorrow. In living out of those wounds, I had often grasped at unhealthy, broken relationships with men in an attempt fill my need for affirmation and soothe the pain of feeling abandoned and rejected. But using men and allowing them to use me didn't solve the problem.

Running from our issues doesn't heal the hurt. In the mysterious plan of God, we must go to the Cross with him in order for true resurrection to take place. As we come before the crucified Jesus and take inventory of our lives, our pain, and our struggles, we receive grace, strength, and beauty. The people who ministered to me in these deep prayer sessions also went to the Cross with me as witnesses, much like St. John the Beloved, whose presence gave strength to Jesus and Mary in their time of anguish. God ministers to our hearts in and through other people.

God is also constantly working to restore the full reality of his fatherhood. Original sin denied the fatherhood of God, but the union of the Father and his children is once again possible through the sacrifice of Jesus the Son. This healing that allows us to live as true children of God is real. When we allow God into the "tombs" of our hearts, a new freedom emerges from his presence. Where once death loomed, new life springs forth. Jesus comes to reveal to us that we belong with him. We have a home in him and we are never alone. We don't have to spend our entire lives looking for a place to fit in, nor do we have to "spend . . . [our] wages for what does not satisfy" (Is 55:2). Jesus unites us to God, who is Being himself, so that we may find our true being and our true dignity. We are made in his image and likeness, and in him we find ourselves.

I don't know what the tombs of your heart might hold. I don't know where you feel abandoned or misunderstood. Maybe you long for a spouse and haven't been able to find one. Perhaps you long for a child and have not been able to conceive. Maybe you are looking for purpose or meaning in your life and have felt empty and alone. Allow Jesus into those places of anguish. You may find that, just as he healed and restored the possessed man, Jesus will come to you to "seek and to save what was lost" (Lk 19:10).

Prayer: Father, thank you for seeing me. Thank you for seeking out my heart. Thank you for creating me to be your child. Please restore what has been lost and broken. Let the blood of Jesus your Son wash over me, cleansing every wound and taking away the pain. May I walk with you all the days of my life. Amen.

Questions for Deeper Reflection:

Answer as honestly as you can and bring your answers, desires, and fears to God.

- Have I taken any steps to begin or to continue along the path of healing? What steps have I taken? Are there any that I need to return to?

- What part of the story of the possessed man from the Gospel of Mark touched me the most? Why?

- How do I see Jesus coming into the tombs of my life to heal me? Do I really believe he cares about me, that he will see me and rescue me?

- Does my life proclaim the Good News of Jesus Christ to those around me? How so?

Chapter 8

Set Me Free

---

*It is good for us to persevere in longing
until we receive what was promised.*

—St. Augustine, *Discourse on the Psalms*

Blessed are those who trust in the Lord*;
the* Lord *will be their trust.
They are like a tree planted beside the
 waters
that stretches out its roots to the stream:
It does not fear heat when it comes,
its leaves stay green;
In the year of drought it shows no distress,
but still produces fruit.*

—Jeremiah 17:7–8

As we journey through life, we are always becoming who we are created to be. In other words, you're never done learning, growing, and converting. Every time we go to Confession, every time we reconcile with someone, every time deep joy surprises us and captivates us with its beauty, we are reminded of who we are created to be. We are meant to live a life of fullness and freedom.

When I was about twenty-seven years old, I surveyed the immense brokenness and unhappiness in my life and knew I needed to change. However, I lacked the ability to do so. Part of me wanted to change and part of me did not. I wanted the bad things in my life to go away, but I wasn't ready to face the painful experiences that caused a lot of my brokenness, nor was I ready to take responsibility for the ways in which I was adding to my unhappiness. I was struggling with clinical depression and self-hatred, and I felt very alone. Even though I was already in religious life at that point, I had brought all the baggage of my past with me.

Religious sisters are people, too. God calls us from all walks of life and from all different backgrounds. We aren't perfect—no one is. We have our own victories, trials, problems, and talents just like you do. Entering religious life doesn't make troubles magically go away. As a matter of fact, living in community usually reveals our personal faults and struggles because of the close proximity of relationships. Sometimes, though, there is a perceived expectation that everyone in religious life must be perfect; the burden of that expectation added to my feelings of shame and pain from my unhealed past.

But through the kindness of many helpful people my life began to change. There was the wise and compassionate sister in my community who first introduced me to the journey of interior healing. There was the priest in Confession who never shamed me but gently encouraged me to consider going to counseling as an aid to healing. There were several counselors who spent many hours listening to my heart without judgment and who never ran away from my brokenness. There were the people in recovery groups who accepted me and didn't mock my struggles or trials. When I was finally able to be honest with good people, the transformation of my heart could begin.

This painful transformation reminds me of being outside in frigid weather and having your hands grow stiff and numb from the cold. When you come back inside and put them in front of a warm fire, your hands may throb with pain as the blood begins to flow more freely. So it was with my heart. Before recovery, it was in many ways cold and numb like those frozen hands. Deep underlying pain drove much of my numbing addiction to alcohol and was the gateway to all the years of cold lust that I lived. But there were many other areas of my heart that I had simply allowed to become numb and cold to avoid the pain of very strong emotions.

As I began to recover, those parts of my heart became warm again, and it was painful to face the feelings. After living so many years with a frozen heart, letting in real love with all its triumphs and tragedies seemed overwhelming. Many times I feel tempted to return to the numbness of the cold, but there is nothing worth trading for a heart that is warm, alive, and appropriately vulnerable. C. S. Lewis writes:

> To love at all is to be vulnerable. Love anything, and your heart will certainly be wrung and possibly be broken. If you want to make sure of keeping it intact, you must give your heart to no one, not even to an animal. Wrap it carefully round with hobbies and little luxuries; avoid all entanglements; lock it up safe in the casket or coffin of your selfishness. But in that casket—safe, dark, motionless, airless—it will change. It will not be broken; it will become unbreakable, impenetrable, irredeemable.[1]

In our pain, we often turn in on ourselves and make vows such as "I will never ..." or "From now on, I will always ..." but these vows are often made in anger or out of sorrow and do not bear good fruit. As we withdraw from real life and real love, our hearts indeed become like a casket and we merely survive rather than thrive. No one, not even God, can force us to give our hearts. That is why the heart of a person is the most precious gift and should be treated as such. As a heart is cherished, treasured,

and healed, it becomes alive and vibrant. I have
seen and felt freedom and healing take place in my
life as well as in the lives of so many other people.
Sometimes healing comes through heartbreak and
heartache, but healing always brings restoration
and life to the heart. We are made for life.

Let me take you into another gospel story, this
one of a woman who perhaps faced a similar situation of living with a broken heart and grasping at
men to try to fill the void. Once again, please allow
yourself to enter into the story and find a place
there. See what Jesus wants to reveal to you. The
Gospel of John is rich in its poetic telling of the life
of Jesus as the Word made Flesh.

Although John recounts many stories in his
eyewitness account, I would like to focus on Jesus'
encounter with the woman caught in adultery (Jn
8:1–11). This story takes place early in the morning
as Jesus begins a day of teaching in the temple area.
A group of Pharisees, the legalists of the day, bring
to him a woman "caught in the very act of committing adultery" (Jn 8:4). Their concern isn't for
the state of her soul or for her temporal well-being
(and they do not bring the other person caught in
this act of adultery, the man). The Pharisees aim to
use this woman (a use not so different from that of
the man who was committing adultery with her) to
catch Jesus in a legal trap so they can collect some

concrete evidence to use against him. But Jesus won't be trapped by anyone.

You can imagine the scene, full of people coming and going about their daily morning business. Many people are gathered around Jesus to hear him teach, and there are also some curious onlookers present. The Pharisees interrupt Jesus, shoving the humiliated woman into his presence and proclaiming her sin. They challenge Jesus to find a way out of the quandary of either stoning her, a violation of Roman law, or letting her go free, a violation of the Mosaic Law.

Notice that Jesus doesn't panic or rush to respond. I imagine him being stopped mid-sentence, listening to the charge against the woman, looking deeply at her, and then silently bending down, crouching low to write in the dirt.

Can you almost feel the weight of the silence while everyone watches Jesus with anticipation to see to what he will do? The silence doesn't last long, as the Pharisees begin to press Jesus again for an immediate answer. Undaunted, Jesus stands up. I can picture him brushing off his hands, looking squarely at the men, and telling them, "Let the one among you who is without sin be the first to throw a stone at her" (Jn 8:7). Jesus then bends back down and continues writing in the dirt with his finger. This moment too is pregnant with silence. No one knows what Jesus was writing in the dirt—John doesn't tell us. Some people say that Jesus may have been writing the sins of these men in the dirt. Whatever he wrote had a profound impact, though, for the men, "beginning with the elders" (the wisest), walk away from the situation one by one (Jn 8:9).

The woman in this scene, who was cruelly humiliated and most likely feared for her very life, is now alone with Jesus. He is the man she has been looking for all along in the depths of her heart. Still bent close to the ground, Jesus looks up at her. As he straightens up, I imagine Jesus catching her gaze as she looks around feeling vulnerable and mortified. Jesus looks at her tenderly and asks her, "Woman, where are they? Has no one condemned you?"

Perhaps she looks to the ground as she whispers, "No one, sir." She has no idea what will happen next; maybe she fears that this man in front of her will be the one to condemn her. But Jesus responds with two very surprising, richly affirming, and life-giving statements.

First, Jesus tells her, "Neither do I condemn you" (Jn 8:11). Imagine the freedom these words bring to the heart of this woman. How often do we fear that God condemns us for our mistakes and sins? We often hide from him out of our own shame and fear. Jesus speaks to the depth of this fear, revealing the desire of his heart. Jesus does not wish to condemn us; he came into the world not to condemn us, but to save us from our sins. Rather than stand back from us and judge us coldly, Jesus takes on our humanity and saves us in his Passion.

Second, Jesus doesn't stop there, but continues to speak one of the most beautiful affirmations given to a human being: "Go, [and] from now on do not sin anymore." I hear Jesus saying, "I know you long for more. I know you long for more than a life of sin, a few fleeting moments in the arms of a man who does not truly love you. You are too beautiful for a life of sin; you are made for more. Go and live a life of freedom."

Healing of our sin is just that, the path of true freedom. It isn't a magic formula or a "fix-it" model. People are meant to be loved, not fixed. The love of Jesus encounters us in our sin and brings us out of it. All the tools he gives to us to bring us to freedom, such as counseling or therapy groups or the sacraments, spring forth from his love for us. He wants his children to be happy and free, just as we want our children and loved ones to be happy and free.

Recovery is a life-long journey. In our addictions, we are stuck in bondage, darkness, and shame. I have learned a lot on this road of recovery, and I still have a lot more to learn. It certainly isn't easy or glamorous, but it's the path of authentic love and life. The people I have met along this path have been imprinted upon my heart. When I become aware of another layer of bondage, and grow weary in the struggle to become free of it, I remember a fellow woman in recovery who would frequently remark, "The question isn't 'What's the least amount of work I need to do?' The question is, 'How free do I want to be?'" The answer to that question lies within your heart. Look within and see.

Prayer: Jesus, thank you for seeing the deepest truth about me. Thank you for the way you care for me and the tender reverence with which you treat me. Give me the courage to continue on the path of recovery, restoration, and freedom. Amen.

Questions for Deeper Reflection:
Answer as honestly as you can and bring your answers, desires, and fears to God.

- Are there areas in my life where I am numb and closed off? What are the areas that have begun to come alive again?

- What stirred in my heart regarding the story of the woman caught in adultery?

- How do I see Jesus looking at my deepest and darkest sins? With condemnation? With compassion?

Chapter 9

Open My
Heart to Love

*In the eternal Father's wedding feast, we
find life without death, satiety without
boredom, and hunger without pain.*

—The Dialogue of St. Catherine of Siena

*Arise, my friend, my beautiful one, and
come! For see, the winter is past, the rains
are over and gone.*

—Song of Songs 2:10–11

Love has an order. I learned this well last year
during the nine months I spent in an intense school
of love while on a year of sabbatical for study and
rest. It's no coincidence that the timespan was nine
months because when the time came to an end, I
had been reborn in many ways. It wasn't an official
university, and I received no official degree when
my time was completed, but that school educated
me in ways beyond my imagination. The location
wasn't hundreds of acres of manicured lawns with
imposing buildings and impressive facades, but a
simple home where a beautiful family lived.

The parents of this family are my age, and the school of love they run with their seven beautiful children changed my life. Living with this family, I watched them love one another, and as I experienced their love for me, I saw firsthand the healing power of authentic relationships. They are ordinary people like you and me who have triumphs and sorrows, dreams and brokenness, but their commitment to love one another as a family, in good times and in bad, releases healing grace to all those they encounter.

Nightly, I watched the husband come home from a long day at work, set his things down on the kitchen counter, and seek out his wife to hug her and greet her. He then looked for his children to embrace and spent a few moments with each one, checking on them to see how their day went. He would fill water bottles for their soccer practice and gather together all their sports gear for the next big game. After putting the dinner dishes in the dishwasher and helping tuck the kids into bed, he would often stay up late into the night working on projects or completing work for the next day.

The wife of the family inspired me daily as I watched her get up early in the morning to help the kids with breakfast and tend to their needs. She homeschooled the children and could often be found ushering them all into the car to take them to guitar practice, soccer games, or birthday parties. She took the kids to daily Mass when possible, and in between the arduous routines of school, meals, and a multitude of events, she would write incredible blog posts and pray with people who needed help. Witnessing the love between the husband and wife and how that strong foundation upheld the entire family changed my life. And I am not the only person they have helped: their entire extended family is devoted to a ministry that has helped thousands of people heal from brokenness and wounds. This is the witness of human love redeemed. This is the restoration of love. Real love is found not in the absence of trial and suffering but in a commitment to the good of the other, whether we feel like it or not.

Real love restores relationships and brings harmony where before there was disunity. This love isn't magic but is the daily work of sanctification. This is the love that a man and woman promise one another on the day they say, "I do." They are saying yes not only to the intense emotion of the wedding day and to the joys that day brings but to every day afterward, in joy and in sorrow. Pope John Paul II writes, "Love in the full sense of the word is a virtue, not just an emotion, and still less a mere excitement of the senses . . . . Love as a virtue is oriented by the will towards the value of the person."[1]

Compare this insight to the prevailing societal mentality of emotionalism in which love is defined as having intense sentiments or feelings toward someone or something. Our emotions come and go. I have had hundreds of emotions today already. Mornings are particularly difficult for me, and something I may find quite disagreeable at six o'clock in the morning may become more palatable by around ten o'clock. Love, although powered by emotion at times, does not consist in mere emotion but in virtue.

Sometimes even the word *virtue* can have a negative connotation or seem outdated and devoid of any joy. Those of us who have grown up Catholic may have heard that we need to be virtuous or to pray for virtue, but many of us don't understand what that means. So what is virtue? Simply stated, virtue is the habitual and firm disposition to do the good. This pursuit of goodness is aided by the grace of God and sets us on a path of transformation, a path to the One who is Goodness. This pursuit requires discipline and hard work; it certainly isn't easy but it's worth the effort. I read an interview with three-time Olympic gold medalist Kerri Walsh Jennings. After all her success in beach volleyball, you might think she would be tempted to feel that she had "arrived" at the climax of her skills and see no need for growth. But when the interviewer asked her, "Is beach volleyball something that you are always improving at or are you like, 'I'm Kerri Walsh Jennings, I got this?'"

Walsh Jennings replied, "No, I feel like I am just scratching the surface! I've been playing the sport for eleven years, and I feel like I am just getting going as far as how much more room I have for improvement . . . . I feel like I have so much more room to grow and I can't wait to be challenged."[2]

A three-time Olympic gold medalist is just "scratching the surface" of her skills? Wow. Imagine if we all pursued goodness at the rate she pursues excellence in volleyball.

On a spiritual level, one can see a greater kind of dedication in the life of Mother Teresa, a woman who tirelessly served, loved, and cared for those in need, all the while in intense spiritual darkness herself. She would pick up the poor out of city gutters and feed and care for the people that society rejected, always affirming the dignity and value of every single human person. This kind of love pours out beauty; it is true greatness that inspires awe in our hearts. It is not a sterile, sanitized version of charity but a fierce, noble pursuit of the divine Lover himself.

These acts of simple, humble, passionate love, performed out of sheer goodness, transform the world. The beauty of such loving service is eternal.

It doesn't die with a person but offers us a glimpse into heaven, which is why Mother Teresa was universally recognized, by people of all faiths and all walks of life, for her compassionate devotion to the poor. She was truly like Jesus; the tender compassion and mercy she radiated came directly from his heart. Goodness and love attract the human heart, for they are our origin and destiny.

As we have journeyed together in this book, maybe you have begun to think about who Jesus is to you, the image you have of him. The image you have of him matters, for it directly influences how you relate to him. Many times in our hearts, Jesus bears the burden of the sins other people have committed against us. We are wounded and in pain, and we believe that God is the source of our suffering.

I have been surprised at how much baggage I push onto Jesus. He bears the scars from the men who have wounded me and from my own self-hatred and rejection for my own sins and brokenness. I see how often I try to manage Jesus by pushing him far away because he seems safer that way. Sometimes I expect the worst from him, or at least total abandonment, when I fail and stumble. During my darker times, I often have an image of myself sitting alone with my back against the wall, curled up into a little ball. I am hurting and broken and feeling lost. I expect Jesus to come and stand over me, hands on his hips, admonishing me for all my faults and failures.

Yet he always surprises me. During these times, he will come and sit beside me, right where I am. He doesn't try to fix me or offer platitudes or force anything on me. He just sits beside me in truth and experiences my pain. His presence is a healing balm, letting me know that I am not alone.

I think the reality of Jesus often shocks us. In one of the most touching accounts of his compassion and humanity, Jesus raises a young man, the only son of a widow, from the dead (Lk 7:11–17). Drawing near the gates of the city of Nain, Jesus is accompanied by a large group of people. He sees a dead man being brought out of the city gates, followed by his mother, a woman with no husband and no social standing. She is poor and needs help, but now her son has died and she is completely destitute.

You can imagine her anguish, the amount of loss and sorrow she has seen in her life as well as most likely a lot of fear about the future (which may be familiar to all of us). Out of the hundreds of people in this scene, Jesus *sees* her. People were always clamoring for his attention, yet this woman, who is probably lost in her own sorrow, is seen by the only one who can really do anything to help her. Luke writes, "When the Lord saw her, he was moved with pity for her and said, 'Do not weep'" (Lk 7:13).

Jesus stops the funeral procession, touches the coffin containing the decomposing body, and tells the dead man to rise. All creation obeys the Word of God. The dead man gets up and begins to speak, completely restored to life.

The people in the crowd, both those with Jesus and those with the funeral procession, are not indifferent, nor do they think the miracle is a "nice event." Luke writes, "Fear seized them all, and they glorified God" (Lk 7:16). The people are terrified and filled with awe and wonder. We've all been to funerals. Imagine yourself at this scene. It probably would have scared the pants off you as well. Jesus isn't just a wise healer, a nice philanthropist, or a homeboy. He isn't dull, mild, or tame. Jesus is the fierce and tender Lover whom death cannot bind or sin destroy. It's often been said that our view of God isn't something so large that it overwhelms us; it's usually far too small.

Jesus sees us all. He always seeks to raise to life what seems to be dead and barren. It was through the dying and death of my father that my mother and I drew closer to one another in mutual understanding and love. When life is stripped of its masks and illusions only a very few things matter. Jesus did not come and touch my dad's coffin and raise him to life on this earth, but Jesus did heal my dad. My dad was healed from the ultimate wound, that of sin and death. I pray to see him again on the hopeful day when I am healed from sin and death and rise to life eternal.

Speaking of my mom, our relationship has undergone a profound transformation since I first entered religious life. What I didn't know at that time was that my mom had been doing something for years that had a direct impact on me— she had been doing a lot of praying! A year and a half after my dad died, I professed my first vows to Jesus and became his bride; and on that day I learned something that changed my life. After the Profession Mass, my mom mentioned that she wanted to talk to me. Dread filled my heart as my mom patted the seat next to her, inviting me to sit down. I feared that she was going to tell me she had cancer like my father, so I prepared myself for the worst.

Instead, she began telling me a different story. She recalled to my mind a time during my college years when our relationship was near a breaking point. My mother, displeased at how I was living my life and whom I was dating, had cut me off financially, reprimanded me, and threatened to disown me. I was headstrong and rebellious and didn't want to be told what to do. During this rift between my mother and me, my dad was silent. However, one weekend my parents came to visit me at college.

It was during this visit that my dad saw for the first time how I, his little girl, was living my life. He said nothing to me but confided in my mom when they got home. Before they fell asleep that night, my dad told my mom of his disappointment in me. Hearing my sweet father speak of his sorrow, and being at her own wits' end, my mother knew there was only one thing left that she could do. She got out of bed and went downstairs to the prayer room in the basement of the house.

In the prayer room was a beautiful statue of Our Blessed Mother Mary. That night, my mom got down on her knees and entrusted me, her wayward and broken daughter, to the care and protection of the Mother of Jesus Christ. My mother placed me in Mary's hands and asked her to take care of me, watch over me, and protect me. From that moment on, completely unbeknownst to me, as I was in college eight hundred miles away living in addiction and open mortal sin, my mother prayed steadfastly that I would become a nun.

And here I am today.

My mother and I have been on a long journey of healing. We have had many conversations and moments of reconciliation. We have shared many tears and much laughter. I believe in the power of prayer, especially from the heart of a mother. I believe in freedom and restoration of relationships. I believe in the power of authentic love. Love, indeed, is stronger than death. Nothing will quench its flame (Sg 8:6–7).

Prayer: Father, thank you for giving me a love that is stronger than death. Thank you, Jesus, for being the very incarnation of this love. Holy Spirit, thank you for being the living flame of love that renews me even in this very moment. Thank you, Mother Mary, for saying yes to this love and, by that yes, changing the course of human history. God, as our hearts are attracted by love, may we come to know you ever more deeply, you who are the source and summit of love itself. Amen.

Questions for Deeper Reflection:

Answer as honestly as you can and bring your answers, desires, and fears to God.

- What "school of love" have you attended in your life? Who has been a powerful instrument of the love of God in your life?

- What stirred in your heart as you read the account of Jesus raising the widow's son from the dead? Longing? Disbelief? How do you think Jesus sees you and the areas of your life that need healing?

- Is there anyone in your life who you need to reconcile with? Who? Have you given up on prayer when it doesn't seem to work? What are some of the ways you have seen God answer your prayers and the prayers of others?

Conclusion

Some of the greatest things in life can pass by us almost unknown. We are blessed right now in the course of history to have incredibly holy, brilliant, and personable popes, successors of St. Peter. If you are around my age, you have lived during the pontificates of Pope John Paul II, Pope Benedict XVI, and now Pope Francis. It will take many years for us to thoroughly study and understand all the rich material these men have written and spoken, but I want to call your attention to a small, little-noticed speech given one summer evening in Germany.

After World Youth Day 2011 in Madrid, Spain, Pope Benedict XVI visited his native Germany. In Freiburg one evening, during a quiet, candlelit vigil, he spoke to the young people who had gathered to listen and pray. What he said to the young people didn't make international headlines, but the beautiful truth he imparted to them has rested in my heart ever since. He said:

> Dear friends, Christ is not so much interested in how often in our lives we stumble and fall, as in how often with his help we pick ourselves up again. He does not demand glittering achievements, but he wants his light to shine in you. He does not call you because you are good and

perfect, but because he is good and he wants to make you his friends.[1]

How often in our lives do we feel that we need to perform well in order to be loved? We feel as though we cannot make mistakes or let our guard down out of fear that we will be rejected. The world always demands bigger and more shocking feats to garner attention, but Jesus requires none of these things. He doesn't demand that we get our act together before he loves us. He simply loves us. In that authentic love is a call to come forth from our selfishness and sin and rise to the true dignity of sons and daughters of God. He desires our friendship and love and gives us himself in exchange.

I hope and pray that this small book on the human person and the love of God has been a source of healing for you. Over the months that I have been writing this book, a certain image kept coming to my mind. Whenever I go to an ice cream shop, I am intrigued by the variety of colors and textures of the many flavors of ice cream. Certain flavors I know well and many I do not. When I want to try something new, I don't usually buy an entire cone. I ask for a sample of the flavor first. What the store attendant hands me isn't a ladle-sized mega scoop, but a very tiny spoon upon which a small measure of the unknown flavor rests. This book is very much like that tiny spoon: it's only a small offering to stimulate your taste for something greater. I hope you finish this book hungry for more of God—more healing, more intimacy, a deeper encounter.

As my mother prayed for me and for my healing, please know that I am praying for you. I entrust you, dear reader, to the merciful heart of Jesus and the beautiful heart of our Blessed Mother. Please know that I will remember you and include you in my daily prayers and offerings from now and into eternity. We are all part of God's family, and that's what a family does: loves one another, remembers one another, and prays for one another. You are precious to God. You are chosen, known, and desired. May you rest in that eternal truth. Let your heart be attracted by Love, the Love that conquers all.

God bless you.

Notes

Chapter 1: Tell Me Who I Am

1. "Suicide Facts at a Glance," 2012, Centers for Disease Control and Prevention, National Center for Injury Prevention and Control, Division of Violence Prevention, http://www.cdc.gov/violenceprevention/pdf/suicide_datasheet-a.pdf.

Chapter 2: Show Me My Purpose

1. Stefano Zuffi, *Discovering Caravaggio: The Art Lover's Guide to Understanding Symbols in His Paintings* (New York: Rizzoli International Publications, 2010).

2. John Paul II, *Love and Responsibility* (New York: Farrar, Straus, Giroux, 1981), 27.

3. John Paul II, *Man and Woman He Created Them—A Theology of the Body* (Boston: Pauline Books and Media, 2006). I highly recommend a study of this work of John Paul II. It is most helpful to study the original text accompanied by a commentary or other resource. I have listed some in the section on Additional Resources.

Chapter 3: Come and Find Me

1. John Paul II, *Man and Woman He Created Them*.

2. Antonio Spadaro, S.J., "A Big Heart Open to God: The Exclusive Interview with Pope Francis," *America* magazine, September 30, 2013, http://www.americamagazine.org/pope-interview.

Chapter 4: Mend My Broken Heart

1. "CDC Fact Sheet: Incidence, Prevalence, and Cost of Sexually Transmitted Infections in the United States," Centers for Disease Control and Prevention, National Center for HIV/AIDS, Viral Hepatitis, STD, and TB Prevention, February 2013, http://www.cdc.gov/std/stats/sti-estimates-fact-sheet-feb-2013.pdf.

2. "Abortion Statistics: United States Data and Trends," National Right to Life Educational Trust Fund, http://www.nrlc.org/uploads/factsheets/FS01AbortionintheUS.pdf.

3. John Paul II, *Crossing the Threshold of Hope* (New York: Alfred A. Knopf, 1994), 228.

4. Christopher West, *Theology of the Body Explained: A Commentary on John Paul II's "Man and Woman He Created Them"* (Boston: Pauline Books and Media, 2007), 178.

5. See www.abort73.com or www.liveaction.org for more information.

Chapter 5: Untangle My Secrets

1. "Child Sexual Abuse: What Parents Should Know," American Psychological Association, http://www.apa.org/pi/families/resources/child-sexual-abuse.aspx.

2. Lynn Heitritter and Jeanette Vought, *Helping Victims of Sexual Abuse: A Sensitive Biblical Guide for Counselors, Victims, and Families* (Minneapolis: Bethany House, 2006), 63–64.

3. Gerald May, *Addiction and Grace* (San Francisco: Harper & Row, 1988), 18.

Chapter 7: Heal My Wounds

1. Mary Healy, *The Gospel of Mark* (Grand Rapids, MI: Baker Academic, 2008), 102.

2. Ibid., 104.

Chapter 8: Set Me Free

1. C. S. Lewis, *The Four Loves* (Boston: Mariner Books, 1971), 121.

Chapter 9: Open My Heart to Love

1. John Paul II, *Love and Responsibility*, 123.

2. Alex Baker, "Keri Walsh Jennings: AVP's Exclusive Interview," Association of Volleyball Professionals, http://avp.com/news-blog/blog/1193-kerri-walsh-jennings-avp-s-exclusive-interview.

Conclusion

1. Benedict XVI, "Vigil with Young People" (Vatican: The Holy See, September 24, 2011), http://www.vatican.va/holy_father/benedict_xvi/speeches/2011/September /documents/ hf_ben-xvi_spe_20110924_vigil-freiburg_en.html.

Additional Resources

Human Sexuality

Butler, Brian, Jason Evert, and Crystalina Evert. *Theology of the Body for Teens.* West Chester, PA: Ascension Press, 2006.

Butler, Brian, Jason Evert, and Colin MacIver. *Theology of the Body for Teens: Middle School Edition.* West Chester, PA: Ascension Press, 2011.

Evert, Jason. *Theology of His/Her Body.* West Chester, PA: Ascension Press, 2009.

Grossman, Miriam. *Unprotected.* New York: Sentinel Trade, 2007.

Healy, Mary. *Men and Women Are from Eden: A Study Guide to John Paul II's Theology of the Body.* Cincinnati, OH: Servant Books, 2005.

John Paul II. *Love and Responsibility.* San Francisco: Ignatius Press, 1993.

John Paul II. *Man and Woman He Created Them — A Theology of the Body.* Boston: Pauline Books and Media, 2006.

Sri, Edward. *Men, Women and the Mystery of Love: Practical Insights from John Paul II's "Love and Responsibility."* Cincinnati, OH: Servant Books, 2007.

West, Christopher. *Theology of the Body Explained.* Boston: Pauline Books and Media, 2003.

Healing

Allender, Dan. *The Wounded Heart: Hope for Adult Victims of Childhood Sexual Abuse.* Colorado Springs, CO: NavPress, 2008.

Eldredge, John. *Wild at Heart: Discovering the Secret of a Man's Soul.* Nashville, TN: Thomas Nelson, 2010.

Eldredge, John and Stasi Eldredge. *Captivating: Unveiling the Mystery of a Woman's Soul.* Nashville, TN: Thomas Nelson, 2005.

Schuchts, Bob. *Be Healed: A Guide to Encountering the Powerful Love of Jesus in Your Life.* Notre Dame, IN: Ave Maria Press, 2014.

Conferences and Retreats

John Paul II Healing Center located in Tallahassee, Florida. Visit www.jpiihealingcenter.org.

Theology of the Body Institute located in Downingtown, Pennsylvania. www.tobinstitute.org.

ECHO Theology of the Body Camp for Teens located in Louisiana and various other locations. www.dumboxministries.com.

Sr. Miriam James Heidland, S.O.L.T., was raised in Woodland, Washington, and is a graduate of the University of Nevada-Reno, where she played volleyball on a scholarship and majored in communications. Although originally hoping to work for ESPN or another news organization, Heidland's life was transformed in a very slow but deep way during her college years. Spending most of her time living a typical college life of parties, sports, and freedom, Heidland seemed to have it all. In reality, her life was empty and broken. Through the friendship of a holy and caring priest, Heidland's life began to transform as she realized Jesus was real and that he was the great love that her heart desired.

In 1998, she entered the Society of Our Lady of the Most Holy Trinity, a missionary community that serves global areas of deepest apostolic need. Heidland has served at missions in Rome, North Dakota, Seattle, and Texas. Her apostolates have included being a director of the S.O.L.T. Apostolic Novitiate for eight years, working with elementary school students, coaching high school volleyball, cohosting a Catholic radio program, and speaking in different parts of the United States and Canada. She is pursuing a master's degree in theology from the Augustine Institute and attends courses at the Theology of the Body Institute.

AVE
AVE MARIA PRESS

Founded in 1865, Ave Maria Press,
a ministry of the Congregation of
Holy Cross, is a Catholic publishing
company that serves the spiritual and
formative needs of the Church and its
schools, institutions, and ministers;
Christian individuals and families; and
others seeking spiritual nourishment.

For a complete listing of titles from

Ave Maria Press

Sorin Books

Forest of Peace

Christian Classics

visit www.avemariapress.com

 ave maria press® / Notre Dame, IN 46556
A Ministry of the United States Province of Holy Cross